THE HOW-TO COOKBOOK FOR MEN

THE HOW-TO
COOKBOOK
FOR · MEN

100 EASY RECIPES TO LEARN THE BASICS

BENJAMIN KELLY

PHOTOGRAPHY BY DARREN MUIR

callisto
publishing
an imprint of Sourcebooks

Copyright © 2021 by Callisto Publishing LLC
Cover and internal design © 2021 by Callisto Publishing LLC
Photography © 2021 Darren Muir; food styling by Yolanda Muir
Interior and Cover Designer: Gabe Nansen
Art Producer: Meg Baggott
Editor: Anna Pulley
Production Editor: Sigi Nacson
Production Manager: Michael Kay

Callisto and the colophon are registered trademarks of Callisto Publishing LLC.

Published by Callisto Publishing LLC C/O Sourcebooks LLC
P.O. Box 4410, Naperville, Illinois 60567-4410
(630) 961-3900
callistopublishing.com

Printed and bound in China
OGP 2

TO SUZANNE AND LLEWYN

CONTENTS

INTRODUCTION

One night, when I was five or six years old, my older sister and I weren't very impressed with what our mother had made for dinner. Our mom was a great cook, but like all kids can be, we were picky. So, we decided to cook our own dinner. Twenty minutes later, we sat at the dining room table, staring down at a bowl of barely warm carrots, potatoes, and turnips swimming in tepid water flavored with cinnamon. That's the first thing I ever remember cooking—if you can call that cooking. I was young enough that I got away without eating any of it. My sister wasn't so lucky. My mom was raising us by herself, and she didn't want anything to go to waste. So, she made my sister eat our gross meal anyway.

Looking down at that bowl, I remember being perplexed as to why it had turned out so terribly. What had gone wrong, and how could it be fixed? Was there a way that it could have tasted good? I wanted to know. My curious young mind was piqued. From that point on, I spent as much time in the kitchen with my mom as I could, absorbing everything I saw, smelled, and tasted. When I was old enough, I started working in professional kitchens, taking in everything I could and working my way up from fast food to fine dining. I even earned my Red Seal certification without having gone to culinary school. All because of one crappy meal.

The majority of my most treasured memories revolve around food. Peeling potatoes while my mother told me stories about her childhood. The first meal I ever cooked for my wife. Countless good and bad nights in professional kitchens. Even more recent memories like feeding my one-year-old son for the first time or watching him pretend to cook with his toys. I'm willing to bet that if you think back to some of your most cherished memories, food was involved. It might be a hot dog at a baseball game. Nachos and beer with friends. Whatever it is, food is always there.

I consider myself lucky to have found my love of food and cooking when I was young. But just because I discovered it early doesn't mean you can't find it for yourself at any age. You don't have to make food your whole life like I did. But if you can find joy in the creation of a delicious meal, I'd say that's a pretty big win.

This book will guide you into the kitchen, where you will develop an invaluable skill that you'll use for the rest of your life. You will learn how to cook food that you can be proud of. You'll cook meals that you will want to eat again and again, as well as food you never thought you'd be able to make. You'll build confidence with every recipe you cook, and that confidence will lead to more success.

Remember, you're just starting. Things don't always work out the way you want them to. Don't beat yourself up, and don't get discouraged. The first thing I ever cooked was a complete disaster, and that led me to this moment. Where will your mistakes lead you?

COOKING BASICS

There is an ancient proverb that says a grasshopper must walk before it can hop. Okay, that might not be a proverb, but it fits here, so just go with it. Before you hop into the kitchen, there are a few things you should know so you'll be geared up for success. In this first chapter, you will learn about setting up your kitchen, the different equipment you'll need, some basic ingredients that are good to have on hand, a little kitchen safety, and other stuff to get you hopping and chopping.

Set up to chef it up

If you don't have the ingredients you need, and if your kitchen isn't easy to cook in, then how will you ever become the cooking genius you know you can be? That's why the first section of this book is all about making sure you and your kitchen are set up to make cooking easy, fun, and accessible.

KITCHEN PREP

Every kitchen is different, and barring an entire kitchen renovation, you go with the layout you have. You make it work for you. Your kitchen should be arranged so that everything has its home. Items like cooking oils, salt and pepper, spices, wooden spoons, knives, and spatulas are best stored beside or near your stove so you can grab them when you need them most.

Know your kitchen. Is your countertop slate or granite, laminate, tile, or butcher block? Can it withstand heat? Can you put a hot pot on it? You can if it's stone. What type of oven and range do you have—is it gas or electric? Gas is more efficient than electric and will heat your pans quicker, but electric is safer. A gas flame is also a little less precise and will heat up the handles of your pans, which increases the chance of burning yourself. Is your oven a convection oven or a conventional one? A convection oven can bake or roast things up to 25 percent quicker than a conventional oven can, if you know how to use it. The point is that you need to get familiar with your existing kitchen and equipment.

TOOLS AND EQUIPMENT

You are going to need some tools to prepare the recipes in this book. Before you run off to buy a new impact drill and nail gun, you should know that kitchen tools are not those kinds of tools. Don't worry, kitchen tools can be just as fun as any other tools. But I'll tell you that if you're just starting your culinary journey, you won't be breaking out the blowtorches just yet. The tools you will need are the basic ones. Let's go over them so you know what they are and what they are for. To keep things simple, each recipe in this book lists the tools you will need to make the dish.

Must-Haves

The first and most important kitchen tool you will need, other than your hands, is a good, solid chef's knife. This knife should have a 9- to 12-inch stainless steel blade that's about 1½ inches wide, with a handle that balances well with the blade. You can buy good-quality, inexpensive knives at any kitchen supply store. A quick internet search will direct you to the nearest store. Don't break the bank on this, though. Buy a knife you can afford; just make sure it's comfortable in your hand; you'll be using it a lot. You will also need a good paring knife, which you can buy at any grocery store for about ten dollars.

You should also have some measuring cups and measuring spoons to make sure that you are using the right amounts of things. It is best not to estimate the ingredient amounts until you have a bit more experience.

Other tools you will need include:

- A large (12-inch) and a medium (10-inch) skillet for frying, sautéing, and searing, preferably nonstick
- Small, medium, and large pots, most with lids
- One or two sheet pans (metal baking sheets with a lip around the edges) for roasting and baking
- A sturdy cutting board made of hardwood, bamboo, or plastic
- A vegetable peeler
- Wooden spoons
- A potato masher

- A cheese grater and/or a box grater
- Silicone spatulas
- A metal spatula
- Tongs
- An electric handheld mixer or countertop mixer
- A digital instant-read thermometer for telling when food, especially meat, is cooked
- A pastry brush
- A colander
- A fine-mesh strainer

Could-Haves

Some items that are nice to have but not strictly necessary are:

- A high-sided roasting pan with a rack, used for roasting meat
- A large, heavy-bottomed pot with a lid, such as a Dutch oven

- A countertop blender or immersion blender, for pureeing soups and making smoothies
- A food processor

KITCHENS ARE FLAMMABLE

Fire trucks are cool, except when they are pulling up to your house because your kitchen is on fire. You should make every effort to avoid accidentally starting a fire. Here's how you can have a safe kitchen:

▸ Keep dish towels away from burners and off the stovetop.
▸ Don't put anything on your stovetop other than pots and pans.
▸ Don't store anything in your oven, especially anything flammable.
▸ Never leave pots and pans on the stove unattended.
▸ Be incredibly careful when cooking with hot oil.

If a fire does happen, call 911, then make your best effort to put the fire out. If you can't put it out, go outside and wait for the fire department. Make sure that you have a charged fire extinguisher handy and that you know how to use it. Never throw water on a kitchen fire, since that could make things much worse. Use a fire extinguisher or do your best to smother the fire with a pot lid or lots of salt.

SHOPPING FRESH

You can't cook without ingredients, so you're going to need to go to the grocery store. It's best to limit your trips to once or twice a week. Otherwise, you'll spend more money than you intend to. But you need a plan. We will talk about meal plans soon; for now, let's look at navigating the grocery store.

Animal proteins (meat, poultry, fish) are typically found at the back of the store. Look for ground beef for quick meals or for when you get hit with a serious burger craving. Pork cutlets and chops cook quickly and are extremely versatile. Chicken and turkey in any form are great for leaner meal options. Fish and shellfish, like haddock, salmon, scallops, and shrimp, can usually be bought fresh or frozen. Unless you live along the coast, it's usually best to buy fish and shellfish frozen. Plant-based proteins, like tofu, are usually sold in either the vegetable section or the health food section and are a way to add protein to vegetarian dishes.

Produce (fruits and vegetables) is one of the first things you see when you enter a grocery store. Buy only what you are going to use and eat relatively soon. You don't want the produce to go rotten in your refrigerator's crisper drawer. Always have things like onions, garlic, celery, and carrots on hand, as well as greens like lettuce or spinach. Fruit like bananas and apples are good for eating or cooking with, and lemons and limes can add a lot of flavor to a simple dish.

Other fresh items like bread, eggs, milk, and cheese, which we use a lot in this book, can be found around the perimeter of the store. Canned goods and dry packaged goods are generally in the middle aisles of the grocery store.

JUST LET IT SOAK: POTS AND PANS 101

Not all pots and pans are equal. Some are made of aluminum, and others are made of stainless steel, copper, or even cast iron. Some have a nonstick coating. They all have benefits and drawbacks. Aluminum pans are inexpensive, but they can react with acidic foods and leach metal into your food. Copper pots are particularly good at conducting heat, but they are expensive.

Cast-iron pans, when treated well, will last a lifetime and be mostly nonstick. However, they are heavy, require regular upkeep, and can be a pain to clean if they get stuck with food. They also may scratch the surface of a glass-top stove. If you do have cast-iron pans, it is best to clean them by rubbing them with coarse salt mixed with a little oil, then wiping them out with a paper towel.

Stainless steel pots and pans are a good option. They are durable, relatively inexpensive, and versatile. If anything sticks to them, you can scrub them or let them soak in the sink overnight. A nonstick pan is good to have, but you can't use metal utensils in it, and you must be careful when cleaning and storing it. Clean nonstick pans with a non-abrasive sponge or towel under running water.

STOCKING UP

Unless you want to go to the grocery store every day, you're going to want to have a few frozen and pantry items on hand to help build your meals when fresh items aren't available.

Frozen vegetables sometimes get a bad rap because people think they are less nutritious than fresh vegetables. This couldn't be further from the truth. Frozen vegetables are processed shortly after being harvested. This means they retain most of their nutritional value, especially when compared to fresh vegetables that have traveled halfway around the world. A bag of frozen peas and carrots makes a quick, nutritious side dish for any meal. Frozen beans, corn, and broccoli are also great when you need a vegetable boost. The same goes for frozen fruit, which makes a tasty snack and is perfect for smoothies.

Similarly, frozen seafood is processed quickly after coming out of the water, often flash-frozen right on the boat. This makes it an ideal option when fresh fish isn't available or isn't as fresh as it should be. One other frozen item that is helpful to have on hand for quick desserts or appetizers is puff pastry. You'll see it a few times in this book, so you'll soon have a pretty good understanding of what to do with it, even though it sounds fancy.

Pantry items like canned tomatoes and canned beans can save you loads of time. Dried beans are better, but they are a lot of work and we're not here for that. Canned tomatoes, whether whole, diced, or pureed, add depth and flavor to soups and sauces.

Your pantry should also have a small stock of dried herbs and spices. Blends like Cajun seasoning, garam masala, Chinese five-spice, and Italian seasoning taste fantastic, are versatile, and can replace five or six individual spices. Dried herbs, like oregano, thyme, and rosemary, are really all you need to get started. Spices like cumin, coriander, cayenne, and paprika are good to have on hand and get a lot of use in this book. Also, condiments like mustard, Sriracha, and soy sauce can all be used to flavor simple meals.

MEAL PLANNING VS. IMPROVISING

If you want to make things easy on yourself and your wallet, meal planning is the way to go. Meal planning means that you sit down once a week and figure out what you will cook and eat that week. You then base your shopping list on your meal plan.

With meal planning, you save money because you are less likely to buy take-out and make last-minute trips to the store. You build into your plan how to use your leftovers, so you save money by cutting back on waste. You plan your meals around sale items. You know what you are going to have for dinner every day, which can relieve stress and anxiety about meals. And, you will know exactly what you need to buy when you go to the grocery store. Even if you are not the type of person to plan, sketching out a rough idea of your meals for the week will help a lot.

WHERE'S A BUTLER WHEN YOU NEED ONE? THE CLEANUP CREW

No way around it: Cooking can be messy. Unless you are the freshest of princes and have a friendly, yet snarky butler named Jeffrey, you're going to need to figure out how to minimize the mess. It's easier than you think. While cooking, keep your sink full of hot soapy water. Whenever you have a second, wash a few dishes, wipe down your cutting board and counter, and clear away any mess. When you're prepping food, cut the vegetables first, then the meat, and you'll need to wash your cutting board only once.

Items like little bowls, measuring spoons, and cups may not need to be washed all the time. After measuring a teaspoon of sugar, you can just wipe your measuring spoon and put it back in the drawer. If you've cut some onion and put it in a little bowl before adding it to your pan, you can put other ingredients for that recipe in that bowl after the onion without washing it. (Just wash it afterward.) And remember to always wash anything that has been in contact with meat, poultry, or seafood right away to avoid cross-contamination.

Prep like a pro

You're in your kitchen. You're hungry. You've got this book open, you are reading a recipe, and blam! You hit something you don't understand. What is a cored bell pepper? No worries, man. That's what this section is for.

TERMINOLOGY

When you start school, one of the first things you learn is how to read and write. Well, take a seat, because class is in session. Cooking has its own language, and you need to learn how to read and understand it. The following are a few key terms you will need to know as you progress through this book. They are not complicated, but they are important. If you are ever confused about what something means, flip back here for clarification.

Boil: If you see "bring to a boil," that means to heat water or another liquid until it is at a full rolling boil, or bubbling like crazy. To boil potatoes or pasta means to cook them in boiling water until tender.

Brown: You will see this quite a bit. It means to cook your food until its surface color has changed to a shade of brown. That shade may be caramel, mahogany, or golden brown; the recipe will usually specify. This browning happens because of a chemical reaction that occurs when amino acids and sugars in the food come into contact with heat. It is what gives steak, pizza, and roasted vegetables their incredible flavors. That's science, baby.

Core: When you have an item like a bell pepper, apple, or pineapple, and you take the center out to remove the seeds and stem, it has been cored. So, a cored apple has its middle removed.

Drain: When you open a can of chickpeas and you pour off the liquid, you are draining the chickpeas. When you see "drain" in a recipe, it means to remove the liquid from something.

Garnish: This term can have two different meanings. It can mean adding an item like parsley to a dish after it's been cooked, so as to make it look nice. In this case, the recipe would say, "Garnish with parsley." But the term can also be used to refer to additional ingredients. For example, if you add lettuce and tomato to a burger, these are garnishes. The same goes for the ingredients in a salad beyond the basic greens. So, if a recipe says to garnish the burger however you'd like, it means to put whatever you want on it.

Mash: You've had mashed potatoes. To mash means to break large pieces of food into much smaller pieces, usually with a tool called a masher. You can also use a fork.

Medium-low heat: If you turn your stove's dial to halfway between medium and low, you have medium-low heat. You'll usually use this temperature for simmering or when you want to slow down the cooking time of something.

Medium-high heat: If you turn your stove's dial to halfway between medium and high, you have medium-high heat. This is the setting you will use to cook most things.

Mix well: This means stirring or whisking something until the ingredients are fully combined. For example, you might put eggs and sugar in a bowl and mix well.

Rest: You've probably heard that you need to rest a steak. All this means is to leave it alone for a little while to help the meat stay juicy and tender. When meat rests, all the juices are redistributed throughout it, so when you cut it, it doesn't bleed all of its flavors onto your plate—the flavors stay in the meat. "Resting" can also be used when talking about dough, but you won't see that in this book.

Rinse: This can mean washing vegetables under cold water or rinsing canned beans after they are drained.

Season: You'll see specific amounts of salt and pepper to use in the recipe, then often you'll be told to taste and add more salt or pepper "as needed." That means to add salt and pepper until it tastes good to you.

Smash: This term is like mashing, but the food is left with some larger bits. Usually, this is done by hand or with a spoon, rather than with a masher, and it's mostly done for potatoes with their skins still on, like Crispy Smashed Potatoes (page 60).

Stem: If you see "stemmed" in a recipe, it means that herbs or vegetables should have the stems removed before you use them.

Strain: Whereas "drain" means to pour the liquid off something, "strain" means to remove the solids from a liquid. When straining, you're saving the liquid and the solids are discarded, unless the recipe specifies otherwise. This is done using a sieve or strainer.

Toss: This means to mix ingredients together gently, as when you toss a salad or toss french fries with salt.

TECHNIQUES

Dice: To cut food into small cubes. The recipes often specify whether the dicing is small (¼ inch), medium (½ inch), or large (1 inch). The easiest way to dice food is to first cut it into slices of the desired thickness of the dice, then cut those slices into sticks the desired width of the dice. Finally, you cut those sticks into cubes.

Grate/Shred/Zest: Grating and shredding are essentially the same thing. "Grate" usually refers to firm foods like cheese or apples. "Shred" usually refers to something softer, like lettuce or cabbage. This action is done with a grater, which can be in a box shape (box grater) or an attachment for a food processor. "Zest" can mean either the outer skin of a citrus fruit or the process of removing it, using a small grater or Microplane.

Grease the pan: This means brushing a pan with a light coating of oil or wiping it with fat. The recipe will usually specify what fat to use; if it doesn't, butter is your best bet.

Mince: This is an imprecise term that means to cut things as small as you possibly can.

Preheat: Before you put anything in your oven or pan, you need to allow the oven or pan to get hot first. Recipes will instruct you to preheat the oven to a set temperature. You turn your oven on and let it get hot for 10 to 15 minutes. Your oven likely has an indicator that tells you when it has reached the temperature and is ready. Pans are a bit trickier to judge because they don't have indicators. But generally, you let a pan preheat on the stovetop for 2 to 3 minutes before cooking anything in it. If there is no oil in it, you can splash a little water into the pan to see if it is hot. If the water just sits there, it isn't ready yet; if the water makes a hissing noise and rolls around on the surface of the pan, it is way too hot. But, if the water hits the surface of the pan and evaporates, the pan is ready to go.

Roughly chop: This is another imprecise cutting term that means to cut imprecisely. Usually, if you are making a soup or sauce that is going to be pureed, you roughly chop the vegetables because no one is going to see them and it doesn't really matter.

Slice: To slice something, you cut it into thin pieces. There's no exact measurement for a slice because it depends on the food. A slice of bread is thicker than a slice of cheese, for example. For the purposes of this book, if you see sliced onions called for as an ingredient, you cut them as thin as you can.

Trim the meat: Most of the meat you buy is going to be cleaned and trimmed already. That means the excess fat and gristle have been removed. But when you buy a roast, you may still need to trim off a little fat. Or, when you buy chicken breasts, you may want to remove the small piece of meat from the underside of the breast, known as the tender.

AVOID THE ER: KNIFE SKILLS AND BURN TREATMENT

Knives are cool and fun to play with, but they can be dangerous. Let's look at a few tips to keep you safe, with your fingers firmly attached to your hand.

Do you know how to hold a knife? Ideally, you hold the knife as high on the handle (close to the blade) as is comfortable. Just like in Little League, when the coach told you to choke up on the bat to get more control, you choke up on your knife. The hand that isn't holding the knife should be holding the food steady, with your fingers up and back from the blade.

A dull knife is a dangerous knife, because it is likely to slip and cause a serious cut. A quick internet search will tell you where you can get your knives sharpened in your town. If you do cut yourself while using a knife, stop what you're doing and deal with it. You don't want to get blood in your food, and you don't want to get food in your cut. For a minor cut, rinse it with water, clean it with an alcohol swab, and put a bandage strip on it. If you have latex gloves, put one on that hand to

Continues ━◀

keep your bandage clean. For more serious cuts, apply direct pressure and go to the hospital immediately.

Burns are the most common kitchen injury. They can be minor, like a little splatter of bacon fat, or very serious, like pouring a pot of boiling water on your leg. Serious or minor, you should know how to deal with burns because in cooking, you will sometimes burn yourself. For serious burns, ones that bleed or are over a large part of your body, go to the hospital as quickly as you can. For minor burns, ones that turn red and are small, run the injured area under cool running water for 5 to 10 minutes, or until the pain subsides. After a while, a minor burn will feel like sunburn, though the pain will be more intense when it is exposed to heat.

COOK LIKE A CHEF

Now that you have a basic understanding of what you need to know for prep, let's move on to cooking. This section covers the cooking techniques for making the recipes in this book and beyond.

TECHNIQUES

Bake: This term usually refers to cooking sweet things, like cookies and desserts. But it can also refer to cooking anything in a 325°F to 350°F oven.

Braise: This term means to cook a food item in a sealed, moist environment. It sounds way more complicated than it is. Essentially, you put some food in a pot or pan, usually you brown it first, and then you add a small amount of liquid, cover the pot, and cook it on low heat.

Broil: Your oven has a broil setting, which turns the top element to very high heat. The broiler is typically used for browning the surface of a roast, cooking steaks, or melting cheese quickly. Because your broiler's temperature can exceed 500°F, the food cooks quickly and so it should never be left unattended.

Mix/Stir: Mixing and stirring are the same process but done with different outcomes in mind. Mixing is stirring with the intent of combining two or more ingredients. Stirring is done to prevent ingredients from sticking to the pan or to redistribute ingredients throughout a liquid, like a soup.

Roast: Whereas a roast is a piece of meat that is meant to be cooked in the oven, "to roast" means to cook meat or vegetables at a temperature between 350°F and 425°F. Typically, roasting is done at 375°F or 400°F. No liquid is added to the food, though oil often is used to coat it beforehand.

Sauté: *Sauté* is the French word for "jump." The idea is that your food is jumping in the pan. This is because the pan is hot and because you keep moving the food. Sautéing is done on medium-high to high heat, so it's essential to keep the food moving; otherwise, it will burn on the bottom.

Sear: This term is usually used for steaks or other meats. It means browning the surface in a hot pan prior to longer cooking. Searing is typically done before braising or slow-roasting to help develop flavor.

Simmer: Some recipes will instruct you to "turn the heat down to medium-low and simmer." That means taking a liquid from a full rolling boil to a gentle boil. It's like the difference between river rapids and a babbling brook. The liquid should still be moving and bubbling. It should just be happening in a very gentle way.

Slow-Roast/Slow-Cook: Slow-roasting and slow-cooking both mean to cook food on low heat for an extended time. These techniques are used for large or tough pieces of meat that will be tenderized over a long period. Think pot roast. Slow-roasting is done in the oven at a temperature between 275°F and 325°F. Slow-cooking is usually done in a slow cooker. Most often, the food is fully or somewhat submerged in liquid when slow-cooked, whereas slow-roasting involves no liquid at all.

THE UNWRITTEN RECIPE RULES

Most recipes are not written for strict beginners. Often, they employ shorthand, and assumptions are made that the reader has some cooking experience and familiarity with terms and techniques. For example, a recipe might say to "add 2 tablespoons of butter," but should that butter be salted or unsalted? Did you know that there is a difference? The name spells it out: salted butter has salt in it for flavor and preservation, and unsalted butter doesn't have any salt—they are sold side by side in most grocery stores. In this book, all the butter listed is meant to be salted. That way, you don't have to worry about buying two different kinds of butter.

When a recipe calls for a can of beans, it will usually say "drained and rinsed." Beans are packed in liquid, so the recipe is asking you to drain off that liquid and rinse the beans. Even if a recipe doesn't say it, assume that the beans should be drained and rinsed. You can also assume that onions, garlic, carrots, potatoes, and the like are meant to be peeled before use, unless the recipe says otherwise. Assume likewise that all mushrooms should be wiped free of any dirt with a damp towel. Recipes that call for meat to be sliced before or after cooking mean that you should slice it against the grain. The grain is the direction that the muscle fibers grew, so cutting against (or perpendicular to) the grain shortens the muscle fibers and makes the meat more tender.

Recipes may ask you to adjust the seasoning just before serving. The expectation is that you taste the food and add a little bit of salt and pepper, stir it in, and taste it again. The salt will brighten the flavor of the dish, while the pepper will add a little contrast. Always start with small amounts of salt and pepper, because you can't take it out once it's in there. The main reason recipes call for seasoning to taste is that it's often impossible to give an exact measurement of salt and pepper, since ingredients don't always taste the same. Two cans of tomatoes even from the same brand may taste slightly different. So, seasoning to taste is done to control that inconsistency in flavor.

Finally, when you are cooking something in the oven, unless the recipe specifically says otherwise, this assumes that the oven racks are in the center of the oven. This position helps the food cook evenly.

Feast with friends

You're learning to cook. That's great. You're probably going to want to show off some of your new skills. You should; you earned it. This section is all about making sure that when you are ready to show off your new culinary capabilities, you know exactly what you need to do and how to set yourself up so you can enjoy the party as much as your guests will.

THE PLAY-BY-PLAY

All right, you've invited some friends over for dinner. Now what? Plan it out. Figure out what you are going to cook. Preferably, it's something you've made before. Trying a new recipe when you have people over for dinner is a risk you should not take. Cook a recipe you know well. You'll be happy you did.

Once you've decided what you're going to cook and you pick your recipes, compile two lists: a shopping list and a prep list. The shopping list will have all the ingredients and quantities you need to buy, and anything else you need for your dinner. Organize your shopping list into categories like Produce, Dairy, Meat, and Dried and Frozen Goods. This way, you can pick up the produce you need all at once, rather than having to backtrack for a tomato after you've already gone through the store. Be sure to include in your list things like napkins, extra hand soap, ice cubes, and something to drink so you don't have to go shopping more than once.

Your prep list, on the other hand, should be a detailed guide of everything you need to get done before your dinner. If you start to prepare a day or two in advance, break your prep list into two days. For example, make Thursday the day when you go shopping and do laundry, while Friday will be for cleaning the house, setting the table, cooking, and so on. The idea is that your prep lists will keep you on track and prevent you from forgetting to do some things.

Your guests will probably want to help in some way. It's best if you plan for a few small jobs that you can assign people. These jobs can be as simple as pouring some chips into a bowl or setting the table. Your guests will feel useful, and that will take some of the pressure off you. Before your guests arrive, have some cold drinks ready and a few snacks set out or prepared to be set out. These preparations will make the evening run smoothly.

The food you choose for your dinner should be something that can be made ahead and then put in the oven or left in a pot to slow-cook. You don't want to spend your whole evening in the kitchen. The less complicated you make the food, the better. Your dinner is supposed to be a nice, relaxing evening. You are not in hell's kitchen, and you don't want to be.

You've put a lot of work into planning your dinner. You've even put on nice clothes. Now open a window and put on an apron. Cooking is steamy business. Whether you are using your oven or you've got pots boiling away on the stove, it's going to get hot. Let the place air out a little. You don't want to be sweaty, and you don't want your guests to pass out from the heat. The apron is there to stop you from ruining those nice clothes with grease splatters or food stains, so use it.

SERVING AND PLATING—OR NOT

While planning your dinner, decide how you want to serve the food. You can serve it buffet style, family style, or plated individually. There are positives and negatives to each option. Let's break down each style, define what it means, and look at when it's best to use that option.

You're a man of the world; you've probably been to a buffet before. So, you know that all the food is laid out in a central area and guests come to serve themselves. This serving style is excellent for large groups and potlucks, or when your guests won't be sitting at the same table. Casseroles, roasts, and salads are ideal for buffet service.

Family-style dining is when the food is put on platters and placed on the table. The guests serve themselves and pass the platters around. This dining style is ideal for when everyone is sitting at the same table and there are more than two guests. Family-style dining is suited to all foods and should be your preferred serving style when having guests over for dinner. It is slightly more formal than a buffet but less formal and less work-intensive than plated meals.

Serving a plated dinner means that you put your guests' food on their plates for them. You have more control over presentation and portion size this way, but it is a lot of work, especially if you are serving multiple courses, because you'll have to get up and down from the table numerous times. You'll also need to clear away the dirty plates from the table before you can serve the next course. Frankly, it's a pain in the ass. Plated dinners are more formal than both family style and buffet, and the effort that goes into them is rarely worth it. Reserve plated dinners for when you have one VIP over for dinner.

No matter which serving style you choose, put some effort into making sure the food looks nice. A few strategically placed sprigs of fresh herbs, a couple slices of lemon, and a little drizzle of olive oil will go a long way toward making your food look spectacular.

EASY WAYS TO IMPRESS

You've put a lot of thought and effort into your dinner, but you're not done yet. There are some small things that you can and should do that may seem insignificant but will pull everything together. For example, you don't want guests rummaging around in your bathroom, looking for toilet paper. Make sure there are extra rolls in a conspicuous place. Maybe even light a scented candle in the bathroom to make it smell a little nicer. If guests are throwing their coats on your bed, make sure the bed is made and your room is clean. Actually, just make sure that everything is clean.

If you are serving meat and cheese as an hors d'oeuvre, make labels by cutting out the label on the package, printing some new labels, or making handwritten labels. You can even buy little chalkboard signs explicitly designed for this purpose. In any event, your guests will appreciate knowing what they are eating. When serving cheese, serve it at room temperature. Serving at room temperature means you should take the cheese out of the fridge about 30 minutes before guests arrive. If you are going to slice the cheese, slice it while it is still cold, since that is much easier than slicing room-temperature cheese. If you give your guests toothpicks to pick up the cheese slices or other snacks, make sure you also provide a place to dispose of the toothpicks. And put out lots of napkins.

Serve chips and other snacks in bowls and on nice dishes, not in their original packaging. It's cleaner, there won't be bags rustling, and it looks much better. Pouring the chips into bowls and plating the snacks are excellent jobs for a guest who is eager to help.

Having the table set before your guests arrive will save time later. Of course, you can always keep this as a job to give to your guests when they ask what they can do. If you don't already have one, invest in a tablecloth and maybe even some cloth napkins.

Set some mood lighting by either dimming the lights or turning off overhead lights and relying on lamps. It would be best if you had some music playing, too. Pick music that is low-key. You don't want dance music blasting while you are trying to have dinner. Keep the volume low enough that your guests can hear each other talking at a normal speaking level.

If you have a dishwasher, make sure it's empty at the start of the night. If you don't have a dishwasher, have a plan for what you will do with the dirty dishes. For example, designate some space in the kitchen where you can neatly stack the dishes for later or enlist a few guests to help you wash them and put them away.

If you've decided to offer dessert, make sure you've made it beforehand, and have it ready to go before your guests arrive. The Espresso–Dark Chocolate Tart on page 163 is guaranteed to impress your guests. If you have a guest insisting on bringing something, dessert is always an easy option to tell them. They can make it or buy a lovely cake. That will take a lot of stress off you. And yes, your guests will expect dessert. No matter what you are serving for dessert, a few fresh mint leaves and some berries will always make a nice plate look great.

THE BEVERAGES

Your guests are going to be thirsty when they arrive, and they will stay thirsty throughout the night. Even if your guests bring their own drinks, which they probably will, you should have a beverage other than water to offer them. You could make some cocktails, like old-fashioneds, or create a fun beverage with vodka and fruit juice. Whatever you decide to do, make sure there is a nonalcoholic version on hand. If any of your guests don't want alcohol, do not ask why, because that will make the person feel awkward. If you serve alcohol throughout the night, or if your guests ask what they should bring, here is a rough guide of what food to pair with what beverage:

When pairing wine with food, a crisp white wine like Sauvignon Blanc or Pinot Grigio goes nicely with salads, cream sauces, roasted vegetables, cheese, and fish dishes. For cured meat or spicy food, go with a Riesling. If you are serving red meat, a Cabernet Sauvignon or a Zinfandel won't steer you wrong. If you're not sure what wine to get, a rosé will go with just about anything.

If you and your guests are more into beer than wine, don't worry. You can pair beer with food easily, too. For salads, burgers, or spicy food, go for a wheat beer or a lager. IPAs are great with steak or grilled meat. Dark ales and porters are excellent with seafood and chili.

If you want to be creative, you can even pair your food with cocktails. Aim to match your cocktails to the region where the food originates. For example, a margarita is a no-brainer for Mexican food, and a fruity coconut rum cocktail is fantastic with Caribbean food.

The goal of pairing wine, beer, cocktails, or other beverages with food is to complement the food, not overpower it or take away from it. If you are going to match alcohol with food, think of the drink as an additional ingredient, rather than as something separate. That way, you can approach your pairings with a little more clarity. When serving alcohol with spicy food, keep in mind that the higher the percentage of alcohol, the spicier the food will seem. Finally, no matter what, always have lots of ice cubes on hand when you're having people over for dinner. Your guests will appreciate it. "Lots" means two to three times more than you think you need.

WHEN IN DOUBT, ADD BACON

You like bacon? Of course you do; everyone does. And everyone loves things wrapped in bacon. When hosting a party, serving one or two bacon-wrapped foods as hors d'oeuvres is never a bad idea. Here's how: Take your main ingredient, wrap it in bacon, stab it with a toothpick, put it in an ovenproof pan, and cook it in the oven at 375°F for 15 to 20 minutes, or until the bacon is crisp. Depending on the food, you may want to flip it halfway through.

What can you wrap in bacon and cook this way? How about asparagus? What about dates stuffed with blue cheese? Chunks of pineapple? Yes, of course. You can also bacon-wrap shrimp, Brussels sprouts, water chestnuts, scallops, jalapeños, hot dogs, and boiled mini potatoes. If you're wrapping a small item like a water chestnut, slice the bacon in half lengthwise before you wrap it for a better appearance. You can also lay some bacon flat on a sheet pan that's lined with parchment paper, sprinkle the bacon with brown sugar, and bake it at 350°F for 15 to 20 minutes to make delicious candied bacon. As the bacon cools, it will crisp up.

Plan to serve some sauces like ranch dressing or barbecue sauce with your bacon-wrapped things. It will give them a boost of flavor, and your guests will enjoy it.

About the Recipes

LABELS

You are going to see a variety of recipe labels throughout this book. They will help you easily identify recipes that suit your needs. For example, if you need a quick meal, look for the 30 Minutes label. If you are cooking for someone who can't eat gluten, look for the Gluten-Free label. You get it.

5 Ingredients: The recipe will have five ingredients or fewer, excluding salt, pepper, water, and oil.

30 Minutes: The food can be prepped, cooked, and served in under 30 minutes.

Dairy-Free: Does not contain any dairy.

Gluten-Free: Does not contain any gluten.

Leftover Friendly: The food can easily be refrigerated or frozen for later.

Nut-Free: Does not contain any nuts.

One Pot: The recipe is made entirely in one pot, pan, bowl, or dish.

Vegan: Does not contain any animal products whatsoever.

Vegetarian: Does not contain any meat.

TIPS

Some recipes offer tips on ways to shorten prep time, easily increase the amount of servings, add additional flavor, or even guide you through a slightly tricky technique. These tips are there to help you and make sure you get the most out of the recipes.

Helpful Hint: Provides guidance when it is needed most, such as the best way to peel an avocado or zest a lemon.

Kick It Up a Notch: Offers easy-to-execute variations on the original recipe that will boost flavor, make it spicier, or elevate it by using fancier ingredients.

Supersize It: Basic instructions on how to quickly multiply the recipe to feed more people.

Take the Easy Way Out: A shortcut or time- or energy-saving tip that will help you prep or cook a recipe or make cleaning up easier.

CHAPTER
2
BREAKFAST

CRANBERRY AND DARK CHOCOLATE MUESLI

Muesli is a mixture of oats, fruit, and nuts, which originated in Switzerland and is now commonly served hot or cold for breakfast around the world. Switzerland is often listed as one of the world's happiest countries, probably because of the muesli. This recipe makes a versatile base that you can use to create your own muesli concoctions.

5 Ingredients, 30 Minutes, Dairy-Free, Gluten-Free, Leftover Friendly, One Pot, Vegan

MAKES: *7 servings*

PREP TIME: *5 minutes*

2 cups quick oats

½ cup dried cranberries

½ cup dark chocolate chips

½ cup sliced almonds

¼ teaspoon ground cinnamon

Plain yogurt, coconut milk, and/or milk, for serving (optional)

TOOLS & EQUIPMENT

Measuring spoons

Measuring cups

Large spoon

Medium bowl

Airtight container

1. **Mix the ingredients.** In the medium bowl, combine the oats, cranberries, chocolate chips, almonds, and cinnamon. Mix them well.

2. **Finish and serve.** For each serving, mix ½ cup muesli with ½ cup plain yogurt or coconut milk and let sit in the fridge overnight. Or, mix ½ cup muesli with ¼ cup boiling water, mix well, let it sit for 2 minutes, then enjoy it as is or add 2 tablespoons milk.

3. **Store the muesli.** Store in an airtight container on the counter for up to 1 month.

KICK IT UP A NOTCH: Add other dried fruits, nuts, seeds, or fresh fruit like banana slices and berries when you serve it.

Sweet and Salty Breakfast Balls

If you want a quick blast of energy in the morning, or any time of day, you can't beat these breakfast balls. They taste great, and they are easy to put together. What's better than that?

Dairy-Free, Gluten-Free, Leftover Friendly, Vegetarian

MAKES: *12 balls*

PREP TIME: *30 minutes, plus 2½ hours to chill and set*

---

1 cup smooth or creamy peanut butter

8 to 10 pitted Medjool dates

2 cups puffed rice cereal

½ cup unsweetened coconut flakes

2 tablespoons chia seeds

2 tablespoons honey

TOOLS & EQUIPMENT

Measuring spoons

Measuring cups

Microwave-safe cup or small bowl

Knife

Wooden spoon

Cutting board

Large plate

Medium bowl

Plastic wrap

1. **Prep the plate.** Wrap the large plate in plastic wrap and set it aside.

2. **Warm the peanut butter.** Put the peanut butter in a microwave-safe measuring cup or bowl. Heat it in the microwave for 30 seconds on medium heat.

3. **Chop the dates.** Put the dates on your cutting board and chop them as small as you can. When you think you've chopped them small enough, chop them a bit more.

4. **Mix the dry ingredients.** In the medium bowl, combine the puffed rice cereal with the coconut, chia seeds, and chopped dates.

5. **Add the wet ingredients.** Add the honey and the warm peanut butter to the bowl and mix well using a wooden spoon.

6. **Chill the mixture.** Put the mixture in the refrigerator for 30 minutes to make forming the balls easier.

7. **Form the balls.** Take the mixture out of the refrigerator and use a ¼-cup measuring cup to portion it. Press the portions into balls with your hands and put them on the plate wrapped in plastic. Cover the plate with plastic wrap and put it in the fridge for 2 hours to set. Store the balls in the refrigerator for up to 1 week or in the freezer for 2 to 3 months. Eat them cold.

HELPFUL HINT: Wet your hands after forming every ball or so. The moisture will prevent the mixture from sticking to your hands and make forming the balls easier.

SEED AND BERRY OVERNIGHT OATS

There is nothing like waking up and having a healthy breakfast ready and waiting for you. It's the kind of thing that dreams are made of. Well, you're not dreaming anymore. This recipe for overnight oats lets you rest easy, knowing that you don't have to think about what to eat when you wake up.

Gluten-Free, One Pot, Vegetarian

MAKES: *1 serving*

PREP TIME: *10 minutes, plus overnight to set*

⅓ cup quick oats

1 tablespoon pumpkin seeds

1 tablespoon sliced almonds

1 fresh strawberry, trimmed and sliced

2 tablespoons frozen blueberries

½ cup plain yogurt

2 teaspoons maple syrup

TOOLS & EQUIPMENT

Measuring spoons

Measuring cups

Knife

Cutting board

Wooden spoon

Small bowl

Plastic wrap

1. **Mix the dry ingredients.** In the small bowl, combine the oats, pumpkin seeds, and almonds.

2. **Add the wet ingredients.** Add the strawberry, blueberries, yogurt, and maple syrup and mix well with the wooden spoon.

3. **Put it in the fridge.** Cover the bowl with plastic wrap and put it in the refrigerator overnight. In the morning, take it out and enjoy.

Coconut, Mango, and Chia Seed Pudding

Chia seeds are these magical little seeds that can absorb 12 times their weight in liquid. As they absorb liquid, they develop a gel-like coating that is surprisingly pleasant. They are also healthy for you. This pudding is so good that you'll feel like you're doing something wrong by eating it for breakfast.

5 Ingredients, Dairy-Free, Gluten-Free, Vegan

MAKES: *4 servings*

PREP TIME: *10 minutes, plus overnight to set*

1 (13.5-ounce) can coconut milk

¼ cup chia seeds

2 tablespoons maple syrup

1 teaspoon lemon juice

1 cup frozen mango cubes

TOOLS & EQUIPMENT

Measuring spoons

Measuring cups

Whisk

Medium bowl

Plastic wrap

1. **Prep the coconut milk.** Open the can of coconut milk and pour it into the medium bowl. There may be a layer of solidified coconut oil at the top; it's perfectly normal. Just add the oil to the bowl along with the coconut milk. Whisk the coconut oil and milk together until there are no lumps.

2. **Mix in the chia seeds.** Whisk the chia seeds, maple syrup, and lemon juice into the coconut milk.

3. **Portion the pudding.** Divide the coconut milk mixture evenly among 4 (8-ounce) cups. Add ¼ cup mango cubes to each cup. Cover the cups with plastic wrap and put them in the fridge to set overnight. Eat within 4 days.

KICK IT UP A NOTCH: To take your chia seed pudding to the next level, add 1 tablespoon cocoa powder to the mixture. You can also add other fruit, like banana slices, blueberries, or strawberries along with the mango or instead of it.

CARAMELIZED APPLE OATMEAL

Quick oats are oats that have been rolled extra thin so they cook faster, which is good because regular rolled oats take a while longer to cook. You've probably had apple cinnamon oatmeal before. Maybe you liked it and maybe you didn't. Either way, you're going to like this.

30 Minutes, Gluten-Free, Nut-Free, One Pot, Vegetarian

MAKES: *1 serving*
PREP TIME: *5 minutes*
COOK TIME: *10 minutes*

1 tablespoon butter

½ cup medium-diced Granny Smith apple (about ½ apple)

⅛ teaspoon ground cinnamon

⅛ teaspoon salt

1 tablespoon brown sugar

1 cup water

⅓ cup quick oats

2 tablespoons milk, for serving (optional)

TOOLS & EQUIPMENT

Measuring spoons

Measuring cups

Knife

Wooden spoon

Cutting board

Medium pot

1. **Preheat your pot.** Put the medium pot on the stove over medium heat.

2. **Make the caramelized apples.** Add the butter to the pot and wait for it to melt and start foaming. Add the apple, cinnamon, salt, and brown sugar and cook, stirring with the wooden spoon, for 4 to 5 minutes, or until the apple pieces begin to soften and the brown sugar gets sticky.

3. **Make the oatmeal.** Add the water, turn the heat up to high, and bring the mixture to a boil. Add the oats to the pot, turn the heat back down to medium, and stir for 5 minutes, or until the oats are the desired thickness.

4. **Enjoy the oatmeal.** Eat as is or top with milk.

HUEVOS RANCHEROS

Huevos rancheros translates to "ranchers' eggs," which pretty much means cowboy eggs. Who doesn't want to eat a dish made for cowboys? This recipe is packed with flavor and is just the thing you would want if you were out wrangling cattle all day.

30 Minutes, Gluten-Free, Nut-Free, Vegetarian

MAKES: *4 servings*
PREP TIME: *10 minutes*
COOK TIME: *10 minutes*

1 (15-ounce) can refried beans

¼ cup water

4 (6-inch) corn tortillas

2 teaspoons canola oil

4 large eggs

½ cup grated pepper jack cheese

½ cup salsa of choice

¼ cup sour cream

2 scallions (green and white parts), thinly sliced

2 tablespoons chopped fresh cilantro

½ lime

TOOLS & EQUIPMENT

Measuring spoons

Measuring cups

Knife

Silicone spatula

Large spoon

Cutting board

Cheese grater

Small pot

Large nonstick skillet

1. **Heat the beans.** Open the can of refried beans and scoop them into the small pot. Add the water and put the pot on the stove over medium heat. Heat the beans, stirring until they are bubbling and hot, 5 to 6 minutes.

2. **Warm the tortillas.** Heat the large nonstick skillet over medium heat. Warm the tortillas in the skillet 1 or 2 at a time for 20 seconds per side. Wrap the warm tortillas in a clean dish towel until you are ready to use them.

3. **Fry the eggs.** Add the canola oil to the hot skillet and swirl it around to coat the surface. Crack the eggs into the skillet and cook for 2 to 3 minutes, then flip the eggs with the spatula and cook for another 2 minutes.

4. **Assemble the huevos rancheros.** Divide the beans evenly among the tortillas. Spread the beans with a spoon to cover the whole tortilla. Put each tortilla on a plate and top with some of the grated cheese. Put 1 egg on each tortilla, then top with the salsa, sour cream, scallions, and cilantro. Finish the huevos rancheros by squeezing the lime over them.

TAKE THE EASY WAY OUT: Rather than heating the beans on the stove, you can put them in a microwave-safe bowl with 2 tablespoons water, cover the bowl tightly with plastic wrap, and microwave on high for 2 to 3 minutes, until hot. You'll want to stir them halfway through, so they heat evenly.

AVOCADO BREAKFAST CLUB SANDWICH

A typical club sandwich has three pieces of bread layered with lettuce, tomato, turkey, bacon, and mayonnaise. This breakfast version substitutes an egg for the turkey and adds some cheese and avocado to bulk it up a bit; plus, there are only two slices of bread, so as to cut back on carbs. But, if you don't care about stuff like that, you can add a third slice between the lettuce and bacon.

30 Minutes, Nut-Free, One Pot

MAKES: *1 serving*
PREP TIME: *10 minutes*
COOK TIME: *10 minutes*

1 strip bacon, halved crosswise

2 slices bread of choice

1 teaspoon canola oil

1 large egg

2 teaspoons mayonnaise

¼ avocado

2 tomato slices, cut ⅛ inch thick

2 leaves iceberg lettuce

1 (½-ounce) slice Cheddar cheese

1. **Cook the bacon.** Place the halved bacon in the medium nonstick skillet over medium heat, and let it cook for 5 to 6 minutes. Then flip with the spatula and cook for another 2 to 3 minutes. The bacon should be browned and crisp but not burnt. Place the bacon on a paper towel to drain some of the fat. Pour the remaining fat from the pan into an old tin can or other throwaway container.

2. **Toast the bread.** Place the bread slices in the toaster and toast to the desired doneness.

3. **Fry the egg.** While the bread is toasting, wipe out the skillet with a paper towel or damp cloth and put it back over medium heat. Add the oil, then crack the egg into the pan and cook for 2 minutes. Flip and cook for another 2 minutes.

4. **Assemble the sandwich.** Spread the mayonnaise on one side of each piece of toast. Slice the avocado as thin as you can and put the slices on one piece of toast. Put the tomato slices on the avocado, then the lettuce. Add the bacon, cheese, and then the egg. Top it off with the other slice of bread. Press the sandwich together gently.

Measuring spoons

Knife

Silicone spatula

Butter knife

Cutting board

Toothpick

Medium nonstick skillet

5. **Cut the sandwich.** Cut the sandwich on the diagonal each way to make 4 evenly sized sandwich triangles. If you like, stick a toothpick in each triangle to hold it together while eating.

KICK IT UP A NOTCH: To add a little punch, add 1 teaspoon Sriracha to the mayonnaise and use pepper jack cheese in place of the Cheddar.

VEGETARIAN BREAKFAST SKILLET

This vegetarian breakfast skillet is perfect for those times when you want a hearty breakfast but don't want meat. It's also great when you have vegetarian guests over. Thanks to the black beans, eggs, and cheese, this dish has all the protein one needs and expects from a big breakfast.

Gluten-Free, Leftover Friendly, Nut-Free, Vegetarian

MAKES: *4 servings*
PREP TIME: *15 minutes*
COOK TIME: *25 minutes*

1 small sweet potato, medium-diced (about 1 cup)

¼ cup hot water

2 teaspoons olive oil

¼ cup small-diced onion

¼ cup small-diced green bell pepper

¼ cup small-diced red bell pepper

1 (15-ounce) can black beans, drained and rinsed

½ teaspoon ground cumin

¼ teaspoon ground coriander

½ teaspoon salt

⅛ teaspoon black pepper

1. **Preheat your oven to 375°F.**

2. **Microwave the sweet potato.** Put the sweet potato in the microwave-safe bowl. Add the hot water, cover tightly with plastic wrap, and microwave on high for 3 minutes. Carefully take the bowl out of the microwave; it will be hot. Puncture the plastic wrap with a knife or fork to release the steam. Remove the plastic and drain the water out of the bowl.

3. **Cook the vegetables and beans.** Heat the medium oven-safe skillet over medium heat. When the skillet is hot, add the oil, onion, green and red pepper, and the sweet potato. Cook for 4 minutes, stirring every 20 to 30 seconds with the wooden spoon. Add the black beans, cumin, coriander, salt, and pepper and cook for 2 minutes. Stir the salsa into the pan and heat for 1 minute.

4. **Bake the skillet.** Take the pan off the heat and spread the sweet potato mixture in an even layer in the skillet. Sprinkle the cheese over the mixture and crack the eggs on top. Bake for 12 minutes, or until the eggs are not jiggly anymore.

½ cup salsa of choice

¼ cup grated Cheddar cheese

4 large eggs

1 avocado, peeled, pitted, and cut into ½-inch chucks

½ lime

TOOLS & EQUIPMENT

Measuring spoons

Measuring cups

Knife

Wooden spoon

Cheese grater

Cutting board

Small microwave-safe bowl

Medium oven-safe skillet

Plastic wrap

5. **Top with avocado and lime.** Take the skillet out of the oven and top with the avocado. Squeeze the lime juice over the mixture. Serve.

HELPFUL HINTS: Dishes will usually say on the bottom if they are microwave safe. If they don't say it, assume you can't put them in the microwave. The easiest way to peel an avocado is to cut it in half, carefully remove the pit with a knife or spoon, then peel away the skin with your hands.

STEAK AND EGG BREAKFAST HASH

A hash is usually a combination of leftover meat, potatoes, and onions, chopped up and reheated for breakfast. It's a great way to use leftovers from the previous night's meal. However, everything is cooked fresh in this version except the potatoes, which need to be boiled ahead of time. To do that, put a potato or two in a pot, cover them with water, and boil them for 15 to 20 minutes, or until you can easily poke a fork into them, then drain.

Gluten-Free, Nut-Free, One Pot

MAKES: *2 servings*
PREP TIME: *15 minutes*
COOK TIME: *15 minutes*

1 (6-ounce) New York strip steak

1 teaspoon salt, divided

¼ teaspoon black pepper, divided

2 teaspoons canola oil, divided

1 cup medium-diced boiled potato (see headnote)

¼ cup small-diced onion

¼ cup small-diced red bell pepper

¼ cup small-diced green bell pepper

½ teaspoon Cajun seasoning

¼ cup grated pepper jack cheese

2 large eggs

1. **Season the steak.** Season the steak on both sides with ¾ teaspoon of salt and ⅛ teaspoon of black pepper.

2. **Cook the steak.** Heat the medium nonstick skillet over medium-high heat, add 1 teaspoon of oil, and cook the steak for 3 minutes per side. Take the steak out of the pan and set it aside to rest.

3. **Cook the vegetables.** Add the potato, onion, and red and green bell peppers to the skillet and cook, stirring with the wooden spoon once a minute, for about 5 minutes, or until the onion is soft. Season the vegetables with the Cajun seasoning and the remaining ¼ teaspoon of salt and ⅛ teaspoon of pepper. Divide the vegetables between 2 serving plates and top each with some of the grated cheese.

4. **Cook the eggs.** Wipe out the skillet with a damp cloth or paper towel. Put the skillet back on the stove over medium heat. Add the remaining 1 teaspoon of oil and swirl it around to coat the pan. Crack the eggs into the skillet and cook for 2 minutes, then flip and cook for 2 more minutes.

Continues ⟜

TOOLS & EQUIPMENT

Measuring spoons

Measuring cups

Knife

Wooden spoon

Silicone spatula

Cheese grater

Cutting board

Medium nonstick skillet

5. **Slice the steak.** Cut the steak into ¼-inch-thick slices and divide the slices evenly between the 2 plates. Top each plate with an egg and serve.

KICK IT UP A NOTCH: If you want to take this to the next level, use leftover baked potatoes, grilled peppers, and steak from last night's barbecue. If you like it hot, slice a jalapeño and throw that into the mix, too.

Sausage and Pepper Frittata

"Frittata" is not only fun to say, but also fun to eat. Think of this as a baked omelet or crustless quiche that tastes a little bit like pizza. You can eat a frittata hot or cold. It makes a mouthwatering breakfast, or even a lunch if served with a salad.

Gluten-Free, Leftover Friendly, Nut-Free

MAKES: *6 servings*
PREP TIME: *15 minutes*
COOK TIME: *55 minutes*

2 Italian-flavor sausages

6 large eggs

¼ cup whole milk

¼ cup heavy cream

1 tablespoon butter

¼ cup small-diced red bell pepper

¼ cup small-diced green bell pepper

¼ cup small-diced onion

2 tablespoons grated Parmesan cheese

¼ cup grated mozzarella cheese

TOOLS & EQUIPMENT

Measuring cups/spoons

Knife

Whisk

Large spoon

Spatula

Cheese grater

Cutting board

Medium bowl

Medium oven-safe skillet

1. **Preheat your oven to 350°F.**

2. **Cook the sausages.** Put the sausages in the medium oven-safe skillet and roast in the oven for 25 to 30 minutes, or until a meat thermometer reads 165°F. Set them aside to cool for 10 minutes, then dice the sausages into ½-inch pieces and set aside. Leave the oven on.

3. **Make the egg mixture.** Crack the eggs into the medium bowl. Whisk until the yolks and whites are all one yellow color. Whisk in the milk and cream.

4. **Cook the vegetables.** Put the skillet on the stove over medium heat. Be careful; the handle is probably still hot. Add the butter and swirl it around to coat the pan's bottom and sides. When the butter starts to foam, add the red and green pepper and the onion and cook for about 4 minutes, or until the onion softens and turns translucent.

5. **Add the sausage and eggs.** Return the sausage to the skillet and cook, stirring, for another 2 minutes. Pour the egg mixture into the skillet and stir for 30 seconds. Stir the Parmesan cheese into the eggs. Sprinkle the mozzarella over the top.

6. **Bake and serve.** Put the skillet in the oven and bake for 10 minutes, or until the eggs aren't jiggly in the middle. Take the frittata out of the oven and let it rest for 5 minutes. Cut it into 6 slices and serve.

CROQUE MADAME

A croque madame is a fancy French version of a ham, egg, and cheese sandwich. Don't worry, you're fancy enough for it, and you're going to love it. But keep in mind that because this sandwich has so few ingredients, you need to buy the best you can find. If you buy good ham, cheese, and bread, this sandwich will be amazing. If you choose low-quality ham, cheese, and bread, the sandwich is going to be *meh*. You deserve better than *meh*.

30 minutes, Nut-Free

MAKES: *1 sandwich*
PREP TIME: *5 minutes*
COOK TIME: *10 minutes*

1 tablespoon Dijon mustard

2 slices sourdough bread

1 teaspoon butter

2 ounces sliced ham

tablespoons grated Swiss
    cheese, divided

1 large egg

TOOLS & EQUIPMENT

Measuring cups

Measuring spoons

Cheese grater

Silicone spatula

Butter knife

Medium nonstick skillet

Sheet pan

1. **Turn on the broiler in your oven.**

2. **Toast a bread slice.** Use the butter knife to spread the mustard on one side of each piece of bread. Put one slice on the sheet pan, mustard side up, and broil for about 1 minute. Set aside.

3. **Heat the ham.** Warm the medium nonstick skillet over medium heat. Add the butter and ham slices. Cook for about 1 minute, flip the ham over with the silicone spatula, and cook for another minute, or until the ham is hot.

4. **Toast the other bread slice.** Put the ham on the untoasted piece of bread and place it on the sheet pan. Top it with 2 tablespoons of grated cheese. Broil this slice for 1 to 2 minutes, or until the cheese melts. Watch it closely because it will burn quickly.

5. **Assemble the sandwich.** Take the melted cheese toast out of the oven, put the second piece of bread on it, mustard side down, and top with the remaining 2 tablespoons of cheese. Put the sandwich back on the sheet pan and into the oven to melt and lightly brown the cheese. This should take about 1 minute.

6. **Fry the egg.** Put the skillet back on the heat and crack an egg into it. Cook the egg for 2 to 3 minutes per side, then place it on top of the sandwich and eat.

TROPICAL BREAKFAST SMOOTHIE

Picture it: You're on a beach, the waves are gently lapping at the sand. A linen-clad waiter approaches with a glass perched on a silver tray. He hands it to you, and you take a sip as a gull calls in the distance. As he walks away, you call to him with delight, "What is this?" He responds, "That is your tropical breakfast smoothie, of course." You can't always be in paradise, but you can always have this tropical breakfast smoothie.

5 ingredients, 30 Minutes, Dairy-Free, Gluten-Free, Vegan

MAKES: *2 servings*

PREP TIME: *5 minutes*

¾ cup orange-pineapple juice

⅓ cup coconut milk

1 medium banana, peeled

2 cups frozen mango chunks

TOOLS & EQUIPMENT

Measuring cups

Blender

Puree the smoothie. Put the juice, coconut milk, banana, and mango in a blender. Secure the lid and turn it on high to blend for 2 minutes. Pour into glasses and enjoy. Beach optional.

KICK IT UP A NOTCH: You can add other frozen fruits to this smoothie, as long as the total quantity of fruit equals 2 cups. For example, you could use 1 cup frozen mango, ½ cup frozen strawberries, and ½ cup frozen pineapple.

Perfect Scrambled Eggs with Cheddar and Chives

The mark of a good cook is knowing when *not* to add something and how to do simple things well. Scrambled eggs are something that should be simple, but a lot of people tend to overcomplicate them. All that stuff is just cover for poor technique. You don't need any of it. Master this simple scrambled egg recipe and people will be blown away.

5 Ingredients, 30 Minutes, Gluten-Free, Nut-Free, Vegetarian

MAKES: *1 serving*
PREP TIME: *5 minutes*
COOK TIME: *3 minutes*

2 large eggs

2 teaspoons butter

4 fresh chives, finely chopped

2 tablespoons grated Cheddar cheese

¼ teaspoons salt

⅛ teaspoon black pepper

1. **Prep the eggs.** Crack the eggs into the medium bowl and whisk until the whites and yolks are combined. The eggs will be solid yellow without any clear spots.

2. **Cook the eggs.** Put the medium skillet on the stove over medium heat. Add the butter and swirl it around to coat the bottom and sides. When the butter starts to foam, pour in the eggs and leave them alone for about 15 seconds. Stir the eggs with the wooden spoon, then leave them alone for another 15 seconds. Repeat this for about 1½ minutes. When the eggs are three-quarters cooked, take the skillet off the heat. The eggs should be mostly solid but still slightly liquid.

3. **Add the cheese and chives.** Stir the chives and cheese gently into the eggs for about 30 seconds to 1 minute, or until they are no longer liquid. The eggs should be tender and fluffy and in big, not tiny, pieces. Add the salt and pepper and serve.

SUPERSIZE IT: You can easily double, triple, or quadruple this recipe by adding more eggs, more cheese, and more chives. The cooking process is the same, though it may take slightly longer depending on how many eggs you are using.

TOOLS & EQUIPMENT

Measuring spoons

Measuring cups

Knife

Whisk

Wooden spoon

Cheese grater

Cutting board

Medium bowl

Medium nonstick pan

HACK IT 5 WAYS

If you want to take your scrambled eggs to the next level, you can try these ideas:
(1) Substitute Swiss, pepper jack, mascarpone, or another cheese for the Cheddar.
(2) Stir 1 to 2 tablespoons of chopped bacon or ham into the eggs to add salty meatiness.
(3) Mix in some other fresh herbs, such as 1 teaspoon of fresh thyme or parsley, to add a load of flavor.
(4) Spice up the eggs with a few drops of your favorite hot sauce.
(5) Sauté 1 teaspoon of minced garlic and 1 teaspoon of minced ginger into the butter for 1 minute, add ½ teaspoon of garam masala (an Indian spice blend you can buy in most grocery stores), and cook the spices for 30 seconds, then add the eggs.

Or, try this: Cook the recipe as described, but leave out the cheese and chives and finish the eggs with 1 teaspoon chopped fresh cilantro. Your taste buds will thank you.

PEACH AND RICOTTA DANISH

Puff pastry can be found in the frozen food section of the grocery store, usually by the cakes and desserts. It is usually sold in a single box with two individually wrapped sheets, so you only have to defrost what you will use. For the best results, defrost the dough in the fridge overnight. Puff pastry is handy for making a quick baked breakfast, a dessert, or even an appetizer.

Leftover Friendly, Nut-Free, Vegetarian

MAKES: *4 servings*
PREP TIME: *10 minutes*
COOK TIME: *30 minutes*

1 sheet frozen puff pastry, defrosted

1 (15-ounce) can peach halves

1 large egg

4 tablespoons ricotta cheese, divided

2 tablespoons confectioners' sugar

1 tablespoon whole milk

TOOLS & EQUIPMENT

Measuring spoons

Measuring cups

Strainer

Pastry brush

Whisk

Large spoon

Small bowl

Sheet pan

Parchment paper

1. **Preheat your oven to 400°F.** Line the sheet pan with parchment paper.

2. **Prep the puff pastry.** Unfold the puff pastry and place it on the sheet pan. Cut it into 4 equal squares.

3. **Drain the peaches.** Open the can of peaches and use the strainer to drain off the syrup.

4. **Brush the pastry with beaten egg.** Crack the egg into the small bowl and whisk it until the white and yolk are blended. Using a pastry brush or your hand, coat the pastry all over with most of the beaten egg. Save some of the egg for the outside edges of the pastry.

5. **Build the pastry.** Put 1 tablespoon of the ricotta in the middle of each pastry square. Top with a peach, smooth side up. Fold one corner of the puff pastry up and over the peach half. Fold the opposite corner up and over, and press it down onto the first corner.

6. **Bake the pastry.** Brush the pastry with the remaining beaten egg and bake for 25 to 30 minutes, or until the pastry is golden brown.

7. **Make the glaze.** Wash and dry the small bowl and the whisk that you used to beat the egg. In the bowl, whisk together the sugar and milk. Take the pastries out of the oven, let them cool for 5 minutes, then spoon the mixture over them. The glaze will set as the pastries continue to cool.

HAM, EGG, AND CHEESE DANISH

Think of this ham, egg, and cheese danish as an exceptionally delicious open-faced breakfast sandwich. It's an efficient and easy way to feed a group of people—or you can keep it all for yourself, because it stores well in the fridge for a few days. Eat it cold or reheat it in the oven.

5 Ingredients, Leftover Friendly, Nut-Free

MAKES: *4 servings*
PREP TIME: *10 minutes*
COOK TIME: *25 minutes*

1 sheet frozen puff pastry, defrosted

5 large eggs

4 ounces ham of choice

¼ cup grated Cheddar cheese

¼ teaspoon salt

⅛ teaspoon black pepper

TOOLS & EQUIPMENT

Measuring spoons

Measuring cups

Whisk

Pastry brush

Knife

Cheese grater

Small bowl

Sheet pan

Parchment paper

1. **Preheat your oven to 400°F.** Line the sheet pan with parchment paper.

2. **Prep the puff pastry.** Unfold the sheet of puff pastry and lay it on the sheet pan. Crack 1 egg into the small bowl and whisk until the white and yolk are blended. Brush the pastry with most of the beaten egg, using a pastry brush or your hands. Save some of the egg for the outside edge of the pastry.

3. **Add the ham and cheese and bake.** Place the ham on the pastry in an even layer, leaving a ½-inch border around the edge. Top with the cheese. Fold the edges of the pastry dough up to create a lip all around. Bake the pastry for 15 minutes.

4. **Add the remaining eggs.** Take the pastry out of the oven. Crack 1 egg into each of the 4 corners so, when you cut the pastry into 4 pieces, an egg will be at the center of each. Season the eggs with the salt and pepper. Put the pastry back in the oven and bake for another 10 to 12 minutes, or until the pastry is golden brown and the eggs are cooked.

5. **Cut and serve.** Cut the pastry into 4 even squares and serve right away, or store in the fridge for up to 3 days.

KICK IT UP A NOTCH: Add chopped scallions to the pastry with the ham and cheese before adding the eggs. Or, switch the Cheddar cheese for Swiss or pepper jack. Or, swap the ham for bacon or salami. And always serve the pastries with hot sauce on the side.

Chile-Garlic Mussels · PAGE 57

SIDES, SNACKS, AND APPETIZERS

TZATZIKI DIP

Tzatziki makes a killer dip for pita bread or fresh vegetables, as well as an excellent sauce for grilled or roasted meat and poultry. Removing the cucumber seeds extends the shelf life of the tzatziki by a day or two. Salting the cucumber pulls excess moisture out of it, keeping the tzatziki thick and creamy in the fridge for up to a week.

Gluten-Free, Leftover Friendly, Nut-Free, Vegetarian

MAKES: *6 servings*

PREP TIME: *15 minutes, plus 1 hour to chill*

½ small English cucumber (6-inch piece)

1 teaspoon kosher salt

1 cup plain Greek yogurt

1 teaspoon fresh or dried dill

1 teaspoon chopped fresh mint

1 teaspoon minced garlic

1 tablespoon fresh lemon juice

TOOLS & EQUIPMENT

Measuring spoons

Measuring cups

Knife

Small spoon

Fine-mesh strainer

Box grater

Cutting board

Medium bowl

Airtight container

1. **Prep the cucumber.** Cut the cucumber half in half lengthwise. Use a spoon to scoop out the seeds. Grate the cucumber over the medium bowl with the largest holes of your grater.

2. **Salt and drain the cucumber.** Mix the cucumber with the salt and put it into the strainer set above the medium bowl. Leave it to sit for 10 minutes, then squeeze the cucumber to remove excess juice. Discard the liquid in the bowl and then put the grated cucumber into it.

3. **Make the tzatziki.** Add the yogurt, dill, mint, garlic, and lemon juice to the cucumber and mix well.

4. **Refrigerate, then serve.** Put the tzatziki in an airtight container in the refrigerator for 1 hour before serving to allow the herbs' flavors to open up. That's a fancy way of saying that it will taste better.

HELPFUL HINT: If you don't have a fine-mesh strainer, you can wrap the salted cucumber in a clean dish towel and place it in a colander. After the cucumber has sat for 10 minutes, squeeze it still in the towel to get out all the excess liquid.

WARM CHIPOTLE, CORN, AND BACON DIP

It's almost game time. You've got some friends coming over. They'll be hungry; what do you do? You get into the kitchen and make this dip. Your team may lose, but you'll win the night. Seriously, though, you and your friends are going to love this dip. And any extra chipotle can be frozen in an airtight container for up to three months, so it's ready, waiting in the freezer when you need it to make this dip again, which is basically a given.

30 Minutes, Gluten-Free, Leftover Friendly, Nut-Free

MAKES: *4 servings*
PREP TIME: *10 minutes*
COOK TIME: *20 minutes*

4 strips bacon, cut into ¼-inch pieces

½ cup small-diced onion

1 teaspoon minced garlic

1 tablespoon finely chopped canned chipotle chiles in adobo sauce

1 (10-ounce) can creamed corn

½ cup grated mozzarella cheese

¼ teaspoon kosher salt

Tortilla chips, for dipping

1. **Cook the bacon.** Put the cut bacon in the medium skillet over medium heat. This is a rare occasion when preheating the pan isn't necessary. As the bacon slowly heats with the pan, some of the fat will melt away. As the pan gets hotter, the melted fat cooks the bacon and makes it extra crispy. The bacon should be cooked for 7 to 10 minutes, or until it is browned on both sides and crisp.

2. **Cook the chipotle and corn.** Use the tongs to remove the cooked bacon from the pan and place it on a paper towel to drain. Pour all the fat out of the pan except for about 1 tablespoon. Add the onion and cook until it starts to soften, 3 to 4 minutes. Add the garlic and cook for another minute. Add the chipotle and creamed corn. Cook for 2 minutes, then remove from the heat.

3. **Turn on the broiler in your oven and set to high.**

4. **Add the bacon and half the cheese.** Stir the cooked bacon and ¼ cup of mozzarella into the mixture with the wooden spoon, and season with the salt.

Continues ◖━◖

WARM CHIPOTLE, CORN, AND BACON DIP   **Continued**

TOOLS & EQUIPMENT

Measuring spoons

Measuring cups

Knife

Spoon

Tongs

Wooden spoon

Cheese grater

Cutting board

Medium bowl

Medium skillet

Small baking dish (6 to 7 inches in diameter)

5. **Broil the dip.** Transfer the dip to the baking dish and cover with the remaining ¼ cup of mozzarella. Broil until the cheese is melted and slightly browned. Watch carefully; this will happen within 1 to 2 minutes. Serve with your favorite tortilla chips.

Sticky Chile-Lime Chicken Wings

You like chicken wings, eh? Fancy yourself a bit of a connoisseur, do you? Well, move over, blue cheese and hot sauce, because there's a new favorite in town. These chile-lime wings will show you who's boss now. Take notes.

Dairy-Free, Gluten-Free, Nut-Free

MAKES: *10 to 12 wings*
PREP TIME: *15 minutes*
COOK TIME: *30 minutes*

1 pound chicken wings, separated at the joints

Grated zest and juice of 1 lime

1 teaspoon kosher salt

½ teaspoon red pepper flakes

1 teaspoon canola oil

2 tablespoons honey

2 scallions (green and white parts), thinly sliced

TOOLS & EQUIPMENT

Measuring spoons

Knife

Wooden spoon

2 forks

Grater

Cutting board

Large bowl

Large oven-safe skillet

1. **Preheat your oven to 375°F.**

2. **Season the wings.** In the large bowl, combine the wings with the lime zest, lime juice, salt, and red pepper flakes. Let sit for 10 minutes.

3. **Brown the wings.** Heat the oven-safe skillet over medium-high heat. Add the oil and the chicken wings, and cook for 3 to 4 minutes per side, or until golden brown. Add the honey, and use the wooden spoon to toss the wings to coat them.

4. **Bake the wings.** Put the skillet with the wings into the oven. Bake for 10 to 12 minutes, or until the wings are cooked. To check that the wings are done, pick out the biggest drumstick, pierce it with 2 forks, and pull in opposite directions. The meat should easily come away from the bone.

5. **Plate and garnish the wings.** Put the wings on a serving plate. Sprinkle the scallions on top, then serve.

HELPFUL HINT: When zesting citrus, use a Microplane or a zester and stop when the zest turns white. The white part is called the pith, and it is bitter. The smallest amount of pith can make a whole recipe taste bitter.

GREEN MANGO SPRING ROLLS

The key to these spring rolls is using an underripe or green mango. If the mango is too soft, it will be impossible to work with and won't have the texture that the rolls need. When you buy the mango, give it a gentle squeeze. You have to Goldilocks that thing—it can't be too hard, it can't be too soft. It needs to be just right.

30 Minutes, Dairy-Free, Gluten-Free, Leftover Friendly, Nut-Free, Vegetarian

MAKES: *6 servings*
PREP TIME: *30 minutes*

1 unripe large Mexican mango

12 grape tomatoes

1 tablespoon chopped fresh cilantro

2 scallions (white and green parts), thinly sliced

3 tablespoons fresh lime juice

2 tablespoons brown sugar

1 teaspoon Sriracha

½ teaspoon kosher salt

6 rice paper wrappers

6 Bibb lettuce leaves, stemmed

TOOLS & EQUIPMENT

Measuring spoons
Knife
Vegetable peeler
Box grater
Cutting board
2 medium bowls

1. **Prep the mango.** Peel the mango with the vegetable peeler, then grate the flesh against the box grater's large holes. Put the grated mango in one medium bowl.

2. **Make the filling.** Cut the tomatoes into quarters and add them to the same bowl. Add the cilantro, scallions, lime juice, brown sugar, Sriracha, and salt and mix well.

3. **Soak the rice paper.** Fill the other medium bowl with cold water. Dip 1 rice paper wrapper into the water and hold it there for 5 seconds. Take it out of the water and lay it flat on your work surface. Repeat with the remaining wrappers.

4. **Make the rolls.** Put a leaf of lettuce in the middle of each wrapper. Divide the mango filling among the 6 wrappers. Fold the sides of each wrapper in toward the center, fold the bottom up over the filling, pull back gently to tighten, and roll forward to seal.

5. **Serve or store.** Serve right away, or store the rolls in the fridge for up to 12 hours, wrapped in a clean damp dish towel.

THAI CHILI–CHICKEN BROCHETTES

Don't let the name fool you: A brochette is just a small meat skewer. Who doesn't love meat on a stick? Whether you are going to a party, a potluck, or a barbecue or having people over, you can't go wrong with these Thai-inspired chicken brochettes.

Dairy-Free, Nut-Free

MAKES: *12 skewers*
PREP TIME: *15 minutes, plus 2 hours to marinate*
COOK TIME: *15 minutes*

FOR THE BROCHETTES

2 scallions (white and green parts), cut into 1-inch pieces

1 teaspoon sliced garlic

1 teaspoon chopped fresh ginger

2 tablespoons soy sauce

1 teaspoon rice vinegar

1 tablespoon brown sugar

1 teaspoon Sriracha

½ teaspoon salt

⅛ teaspoon black pepper

1 pound skinless, boneless chicken thighs, cut into ½-inch cubes

½ lime

1. **Make the chicken.** In the medium bowl, combine the scallions, garlic, ginger, soy sauce, rice vinegar, brown sugar, Sriracha, salt, and pepper. Mix it well. Add the cubed chicken and stir to make sure it is coated in the marinade. Cover the bowl with plastic wrap and put it in the fridge for 2 hours. Meanwhile, put the skewers in the large cup and cover them with water. Let them soak for 1 hour.

2. **Make the sauce.** In a small pot, combine the soy sauce, brown sugar, rice vinegar, and water. Bring to a boil over high heat and cook for 2 minutes. Take the pot off the heat and set aside.

3. **Prep the oven.** Before you start skewering the chicken, adjust your oven racks so that the top rack is in the middle of the oven. Turn on the broiler in your oven to high heat.

4. **Skewer the chicken.** Take the marinated chicken out of the fridge. Drain the skewers and put 3 to 4 pieces of chicken on each skewer. Put the skewered chicken on the rack of the broiler pan.

5. **Broil the chicken.** Broil the chicken for 5 minutes. Take the pan out of the oven, flip the skewers over, and brush them with some of the sauce. Put the chicken back under the broiler for 3 more minutes. Flip the skewers again and brush them with the remaining sauce, then broil for 4 more minutes, or until they start to brown.

Continues ━━◁

FOR THE SAUCE

2 tablespoons soy sauce

2 tablespoons brown sugar

1 teaspoon rice vinegar

2 tablespoons water

TOOLS & EQUIPMENT

Measuring spoons

Knife

Wooden spoon

Pastry brush

Tongs

Cutting board

Medium bowl

Large (12-ounce) cup

12 (4-inch) bamboo skewers

Small pot

Broiler pan with rack

Plastic wrap

6. **Serve the chicken.** Put the chicken skewers on a serving plate, squeeze the lime juice over them, and serve.

SUPERSIZE IT: These skewers are a great choice for a potluck or barbecue. Luckily, you can double or quadruple this recipe easily. What's more, the sauce can be made a day or two ahead, and the chicken can be marinated and skewered a day ahead.

ROASTED EGGPLANT DIP WITH YOGURT AND MINT

This is a straightforward, delicious recipe. The flesh of the eggplant essentially lique-fies as it cooks, making the perfect dip for warm pita breads. This recipe can easily be made on the grill as well; just brush the eggplant with a little oil, place it on a hot grill, and forget about it for 45 minutes. That's it, I swear.

5 Ingredients, Nut-Free, One Pot, Vegetarian

MAKES: *6 servings*
PREP TIME: *5 minutes*
COOK TIME: *45 minutes*

1 large eggplant

3 teaspoons olive oil, divided

6 small pita breads

2 tablespoons plain yogurt

½ teaspoon salt

1 tablespoon chopped fresh mint

½ lemon

TOOLS & EQUIPMENT

Measuring spoons

Knife

Cutting board

Small roasting pan

Aluminum foil

1. **Preheat your oven to 400°F.**

2. **Roast the eggplant.** Put the eggplant in a small roasting pan and drizzle with 2 teaspoons of olive oil. Roast for 35 minutes, flipping halfway through. Take the eggplant out of the oven and let it rest for 10 minutes. Keep the oven on.

3. **Warm the pita breads.** Wrap the pitas in aluminum foil and put them in the oven to warm for 10 minutes.

4. **Make the dip.** Leave the eggplant in the roasting pan, or put it on a small plate or serving platter. Cut off the stem end, then cut the eggplant lengthwise and open it up like a book. Top it with the remaining 1 teaspoon of olive oil, the yogurt, salt, and mint. Squeeze the lemon juice over the eggplant and serve with the warm pita breads for dipping.

Oven-Baked Onion Rings

Imagine you're walking down the street. A guy walks up to you and tells you that onion rings don't have to be bad for you. You can bake them in the oven, and they'll be better than deep-fried, he says. You'd laugh right in his face and keep on walking. Well, my friend, you should have listened, because it's true. Now wipe that tear of joy from your eye and get in the kitchen, 'cause you got some onion rings to eat.

5 Ingredients, Dairy-Free, Nut-Free, Vegetarian

MAKES: *2 servings*
PREP TIME: *25 minutes*
COOK TIME: *25 minutes*

½ cup olive oil, divided

2 baseball-size onions

1½ teaspoons kosher salt, divided

½ cup all-purpose flour

⅛ teaspoon black pepper

2 large eggs

1 cup fine bread crumbs

TOOLS & EQUIPMENT

Measuring spoons

Measuring cups

Knife

Whisk

Tongs

Cutting board

Medium bowl

3 small bowls

Sheet pan

1. **Preheat your oven to 375°F.** Spread ¼ cup of the olive oil on the sheet pan.

2. **Prep the onions.** Slice the onions into ¼-inch-thick rounds. Pull the rings apart.

3. **Salt the onions.** Put the onion rings in the medium bowl with ¾ teaspoon of salt. Toss the rings to coat them well and let them sit for 10 minutes.

4. **Set up your breading station.** Set out 3 small bowls. Put the flour in the first bowl and season it with the remaining ¾ teaspoon of salt and the pepper. Crack the eggs into the second bowl and whisk until the yolks and whites are combined. Put the bread crumbs in the third bowl.

5. **Bread the onion rings.** Take a few onion rings at a time and roll in the flour, then dip in the egg, then dust with the breadcrumbs. With each coating, make sure to shake off any excess before moving on to the next bowl. When the rings have been breaded, place them on the oiled sheet pan in a single layer. Repeat until all the rings have been breaded. Make sure to bread any small pieces of onion as well, as they often end up being the tastiest bits.

6. **Cook the rings.** Bake the onion rings for 15 minutes. Take them out, flip them with the tongs, and return to the oven to cook for 10 more minutes, until crispy. Serve.

KICK IT UP A NOTCH: For a little spice, add ½ teaspoon cayenne to the flour mixture.

STEAK AND ROASTED PEPPER NACHOS WITH AVOCADO CREMA

Are you prepared for what's about to happen? Get ready, because once you taste these nachos, you will never look at a plate of bar nachos the same way again. There are two secrets to otherworldly nachos: (1) spread the chips out in one layer so they all get cheese and toppings; (2) precook your ingredients because they taste better that way. It's that simple.

Gluten-Free, Nut-Free

MAKES: *6 servings*
PREP TIME: *20 minutes*
COOK TIME: *50 minutes*

---

1 green bell pepper

1 red bell pepper

1 jalapeño

1 baseball-size onion

3 teaspoons olive oil, divided

2 teaspoons kosher salt, divided

¾ teaspoon black pepper, divided

1 ripe avocado

2 teaspoons fresh lime juice

½ cup sour cream

1 (8-ounce) New York strip steak

1 (13-ounce) bag tortilla chips

1 cup grated Cheddar cheese

1 cup grated pepper jack cheese

Salsa of choice

1. **Preheat your oven to 400°F.** Line the sheet pan with parchment paper.

2. **Prep the peppers and onion.** Cut the bell peppers and the jalapeño in half and remove the seeds and stems. Cut into ¼-inch slices. Cut the onion in half and then into ¼-inch half-moon slices. Put the bell peppers, jalapeño, and onion in the large bowl along with 2 teaspoons of olive oil, 1 teaspoon of salt, and ¼ teaspoon of pepper. Mix with your hands to coat the peppers and onion with the oil, then spread them out on the lined sheet pan.

3. **Roast the vegetables.** Place the vegetables in the oven and roast for 30 minutes. Take them out of the oven, let them cool for 10 minutes, then dice into ¼-inch cubes. When cool, put the diced peppers and onion in a bowl and set aside. Keep the oven on.

4. **Make the avocado crema.** Peel and pit the avocado. Using a fork, mash the avocado in the small bowl with the lime juice, and add another ¼ teaspoon of salt. Add the sour cream and mix well. Cover with plastic wrap and set aside.

Continues ➤

STEAK AND ROASTED PEPPER NACHOS   Continued

TOOLS & EQUIPMENT

Measuring spoons

Measuring cups

Knife

Fork

Cheese grater

Cutting board

Large bowl

Small bowl

Sheet pan

Medium skillet

Parchment paper

Plastic wrap

5. **Cook the steak.** Heat the medium skillet over medium-high heat. Season the steak with the remaining ¾ teaspoon of salt and remaining ½ teaspoon of black pepper. Add the remaining 1 teaspoon of olive oil to the pan, let it get hot, and then cook the steak for 2 minutes per side. Rest the steak for 5 minutes, then slice it against the grain (see page 14 for details).

6. **Make the nachos.** Put a fresh piece of parchment paper on the sheet pan you used to roast the peppers. Spread the tortilla chips in a single layer on the sheet pan. Cover the chips with half the cheeses. Top with the peppers and onion, slices of the steak, and then the remaining cheeses. Bake for 10 minutes.

7. **Serve the nachos.** Serve with the avocado crema and your favorite salsa on the side.

HELPFUL HINT: You can roast and dice the peppers, precook the steak, and make the avocado crema a day ahead. That way, if you have friends coming over to watch the newest superhero movie or the big game, it will take you only a few minutes to throw the nachos together.

Chile-Garlic Mussels

Mussels make a quick and delicious starter for a multi-course meal. Buy mussels fresh the day you are going to use them, and cook them right before serving. Mussels are a premium source of selenium, vitamin B_{12}, and zinc. They taste amazing and are good for you. You can't go wrong.

30 Minutes, Gluten-Free, Nut-Free, One Pot

MAKES: *2 servings*
PREP TIME: *10 minutes*
COOK TIME: *10 minutes*

2 teaspoons olive oil

1 teaspoon sliced garlic

½ teaspoon red pepper flakes

2 pounds cleaned mussels

¼ cup dry white wine

1 tablespoon butter

2 teaspoons fresh lemon juice

TOOLS & EQUIPMENT

Measuring spoons

Measuring cups

Knife

Large spoon

Cutting board

Large pot with lid

1. **Heat the large pot over medium-high heat.**

2. **Cook the garlic.** Add the oil, garlic, and red pepper flakes to the pot and cook for 1 minute.

3. **Cook the mussels and white wine.** Add the mussels and wine to the pot and cover with the lid. Cook for 4 to 5 minutes, or until all the mussels are wide open. Give any unopened mussels a poke, and if they do not open, discard them.

4. **Finish with butter and lemon juice.** Add the butter and lemon juice to the pot. Stir the mussels until the butter melts, then serve.

HELPFUL HINT: Fresh mussels, which are often sold in net bags so you can't really examine them, should be closed; if any of them are open, they should close when you tap them gently on a hard surface. Discard any mussels that don't close or that have broken shells. Remember that mussels are alive when you buy them, so don't store them in a sealed bag, since they will suffocate. Also, they are saltwater bivalves, so don't submerge them in freshwater for more than a minute—that will kill them. Clean the mussels by running them under cold water, brushing away any remaining dirt, and pulling off any lingering beards. Today, most mussels are farm-raised and sold already cleaned and debearded.

MEXICAN-STYLE CHEESY RICE

This Mexican-style rice is an ideal side dish for grilled or roasted meat, fish, or poultry. It also makes a tasty filling for stuffed peppers (such as the ones on page 135) and burritos. For a pop of chopped fresh flavor, mix 2 tablespoons of fresh cilantro into the finished rice.

Gluten-Free, Leftover Friendly, Nut-Free, One Pot, Vegetarian

MAKES: *4 servings*
PREP TIME: *10 minutes*
COOK TIME: *25 minutes*

1 tablespoon olive oil
2 scallions (white and green parts), cut into ¼-inch dice
1 teaspoon sliced garlic
1 teaspoon dried oregano
1 teaspoon chili powder
¼ teaspoon kosher salt
⅛ teaspoon black pepper
½ cup jasmine rice
¼ cup salsa of choice
¾ cup water
½ cup grated pepper jack cheese
Juice of ½ lime

TOOLS & EQUIPMENT

Measuring cups/spoons
Knife
Fork
Wooden spoon
Cheese grater
Cutting board
Medium pot with lid

1. **Heat the medium pot over medium-high heat.**

2. **Cook the rice.** Add the olive oil, scallions, and garlic to the pot and cook for 2 minutes. Add the oregano, chili powder, salt, pepper, rice, and salsa and cook, stirring for 2 minutes. Add the water and gently stir with the wooden spoon to ensure that no rice is stuck to the bottom of the pot. Bring to a boil, cover with the lid, turn the heat down to low, and simmer for 17 minutes. Take the pot off the heat and let it sit, covered, for 5 minutes.

3. **Finish the rice.** Fluff the rice with a fork, then stir in the cheese and sprinkle with the lime juice. Serve.

Italian Roasted Vegetables

Whether you are looking for a go-to side dish or want some veggies to throw into a wrap or a salad, look no further. These roasted vegetables are like the Swiss Army knife of vegetable dishes—infinitely applicable. If you want to change it a bit, you can add other vegetables like sweet potatoes, butternut squash, or onions to the mix.

5 Ingredients, Dairy-Free, Gluten-Free, Leftover Friendly, Nut-Free, Vegan

MAKES: *6 servings*
PREP TIME: *15 minutes*
COOK TIME: *30 minutes*

1 large green bell pepper

1 large red bell pepper

1 medium zucchini

1 cup grape tomatoes

1 tablespoon dried
   Italian seasoning

½ teaspoon salt

¼ teaspoon black pepper

3 tablespoons olive oil

TOOLS & EQUIPMENT

Measuring spoons

Measuring cups

Knife

Cutting board

Large bowl

Sheet pan

Parchment paper

1. **Preheat your oven to 400°F.** Line the sheet pan with parchment paper.

2. **Dice the peppers.** Cut the red and green bell peppers in half and remove the seeds and stems. Cut the peppers into 1-inch-thick slices, then cut those slices into 1-inch squares. Put the cut peppers in the large bowl.

3. **Dice the zucchini.** Trim the stem and tip end off the zucchini. Cut it into quarters crosswise, then cut the quarters into 1-inch pieces; add to the bowl.

4. **Toss the vegetables with oil and seasoning.** Add the grape tomatoes to the bowl along with the Italian seasoning, salt, pepper, and olive oil. Toss the vegetables with your hands to coat everything with oil and seasoning.

5. **Roast the vegetables.** Spread the vegetables in an even layer on the parchment-lined sheet pan. Roast for 20 minutes, then stir and cook for another 10 minutes. Serve.

CRISPY SMASHED POTATOES

Let's face it, the only thing in this world better than crispy potatoes is getting to smash stuff. Well, now you can have both at the same time, because this recipe combines the joy of smashing things with the pleasure of delicious, crispy potatoes. Serve the potatoes as a side dish, or top with melted cheese, bacon bits, sour cream, and scallions for a delicious loaded snack.

5 Ingredients, Dairy-Free, Gluten-Free, Leftover Friendly, Nut-Free, Vegan

MAKES: *6 servings*
PREP TIME: *5 minutes*
COOK TIME: *55 minutes*

1½ pounds baby
   yellow potatoes
¼ cup olive oil
½ teaspoon kosher salt
⅛ teaspoon black pepper

TOOLS & EQUIPMENT

Measuring spoons
Measuring cups
Spoon
Fork
Colander
Large pot
Sheet pan

1. **Preheat your oven to 400°F.**

2. **Boil the potatoes.** Put the potatoes in the large pot and cover with water. Put the pot over high heat and bring the water to a boil. Cook the potatoes for about 20 minutes, or until you can easily poke a fork through them. Drain the potatoes in the colander and let them sit for 10 minutes.

3. **Roast the potatoes.** Coat the sheet pan with the olive oil. Put the potatoes in the pan, leaving a ½-inch space between them, and press them down with the back of a spoon to flatten them. Season the potatoes with the salt and pepper. Roast the potatoes for 35 minutes, flipping halfway through. The potatoes are done when they are crispy on both sides.

Perfect Mashed Potatoes

It may seem unnecessary to include a recipe for mashed potatoes in a cookbook. Pretty much everyone has made or has seen someone make mashed potatoes. But here's the thing: There are mashed potatoes, and then there are *mashed potatoes*. These mashed potatoes are not the lumpy, bland glop you get in a diner or at a sad Thanksgiving. No matter what else is on the plate, these mashed potatoes will be the star of the show.

5 Ingredients, 30 Minutes, Gluten-Free, Nut-Free, One Pot, Vegetarian

MAKES: *4 servings*
PREP TIME: *5 minutes*
COOK TIME: *15 minutes*

1 pound yellow-fleshed potatoes, such as Yukon Gold

2 teaspoons salt, divided, plus more as needed

2 tablespoons butter

½ cup heavy cream

¼ teaspoon black pepper, or more as needed

TOOLS & EQUIPMENT

Measuring spoons

Measuring cups

Knife

Vegetable peeler

Potato masher

Cutting board

Colander

Medium pot

1. **Prep the potatoes.** Peel the potatoes and cut them into 1-inch cubes. Rinse the potatoes under cold water until the water runs clear.

2. **Boil the potatoes.** Put the potatoes in the medium pot, add water to cover, and add 1 teaspoon of salt. Put the pot on the stove over high heat and bring to a boil. Cook for 12 minutes, or until the potatoes are soft, then drain in the colander.

3. **Heat the cream and butter.** Put the pot back on the stove and add the butter, cream, pepper, and remaining 1 teaspoon of salt. Turn the heat to medium and warm the mixture until the cream starts to boil. Take the pot off the heat and add the cooked potatoes.

4. **Mash the potatoes.** Off the heat, mash the potatoes until they are smooth. Taste them, then add a little more salt and pepper if needed.

Continues ➤

HACK IT 5 WAYS

The cool thing about mashed potatoes is how versatile they are. You can use this basic recipe to create an infinite number of flavor combinations. Here are five such variations that are easy to do and that you will love:

(1) Mix ¼ cup of thinly sliced scallions into the potatoes and serve with fried chicken or steak.

(2) Mix 1 tablespoon of sour cream, 2 tablespoons of grated Cheddar cheese, 2 tablespoons of crispy bacon bits, and 1 tablespoon of minced fresh chives into the potatoes for a loaded-baked potato flavor.

(3) Add 4 garlic cloves to the pot when boiling the potatoes, then mash the garlic right along with the potatoes for a nice, mild, garlicky flavor.

(4) Mix ¼ cup of fried onions into the mashed potatoes for a great sweet onion flavor.

(5) Sauté 1 teaspoon of minced garlic in the butter before adding the cream, then warm the cream, mash the potatoes, and add 3 tablespoons grated Parmesan cheese.

MAPLE AND BROWN BUTTER HASSELBACK SWEET POTATOES

"Hasselback" means to make multiple, even slices partway through a food to create more surface area. The key here is that you don't slice all the way through the sweet potatoes. You want them to stay together when cooked. It's a lot easier than it sounds, and it looks impressive when you serve it. These sweet potatoes are fantastic as a side dish for any holiday meal or with roasted pork or chicken.

5 Ingredients, Gluten-Free, Nut-Free, Vegetarian

MAKES: *4 servings*
PREP TIME: *10 minutes*
COOK TIME: *1 hour 25 minutes*

2 sweet potatoes about the same size

2 teaspoons olive oil

¼ teaspoon kosher salt

⅛ teaspoon black pepper

½ cup water, divided

2 tablespoons butter

¼ cup maple syrup

½ teaspoon apple cider vinegar

1. **Preheat your oven to 375°F.**

2. **Clean the sweet potatoes.** Wash the sweet potatoes under cold running water, then pat dry with a clean dish towel or paper towel.

3. **Hasselback the potatoes.** Put the 2 wooden spoons parallel to each other on your cutting board; place 1 sweet potato snuggly between them. Slice the potato crosswise, straight down to about ¼ inch from the bottom. The wooden spoons should stop your knife so you don't cut all the way through the potato. Make ¼-inch slices down the length of each potato.

4. **Roast the potatoes.** Gently rub the olive oil over the surface of the sweet potatoes, then season them with the salt and pepper. Put the sweet potatoes in the small roasting pan, then pour ¼ cup of water into the pan. Cover with foil and bake for 40 minutes.

5. **Make the sauce.** Melt the butter in a small pot over medium heat. Continue to cook the butter for 1½ to 2 minutes, or until it starts to brown. Add the maple syrup and the remaining ¼ cup of water and cook for another 2 minutes. Add the vinegar and cook for 2 more minutes, then remove the pot from the heat and set aside.

Continues ━⋲

MAPLE AND BROWN BUTTER HASSELBACK SWEET POTATOES Continued

TOOLS & EQUIPMENT

Measuring spoons

Measuring cups

Knife

2 wooden spoons

Large spoon

Fork

Cutting board

Small pot

Small roasting pan

Aluminum foil

6. **Baste the potatoes.** Take the sweet potatoes out of the oven and remove the foil. Spoon one-third of the maple–brown butter mixture over the potatoes, then put them back in the oven, uncovered, for 15 minutes more. Repeat 2 more times, or until a fork easily pokes into the potatoes.

7. **Serve.** Plate the sweet potatoes on a small platter, then pour the liquid from the roasting pan over them.

SUPERSIZE IT: You can easily multiply this recipe by using more sweet potatoes and increasing the ingredient volumes for the sauce. If you are making this for a group of people, use small sweet potatoes so that everyone gets their own. Small potatoes also cut down on the baking time.

BRAISED RED CABBAGE WITH APPLE

You're probably skimming through this book right now, picking out the recipes that you want to try first. You likely saw this recipe and thought you'd skip right by it. Then this paragraph caught your eye, and now you're reading this. Good, because you should not skip this recipe. It is a fantastic side dish for pork chops, scallops, white fish, and even roast chicken. This may even end up being one of your favorite recipes in the whole book. Cabbage: Who knew?

Dairy-Free, Gluten-Free, Leftover Friendly, Nut-Free, One Pot

MAKES: *6 servings*
PREP TIME: *15 minutes*
COOK TIME: *30 minutes*

½ cup large-diced bacon (4 slices)

4 cups grated red cabbage

1 cup grated Granny Smith apple

1 cup sliced onion

1 teaspoon sliced garlic

½ teaspoon salt

⅛ teaspoon black pepper

2 tablespoons honey

1 cup hot water

2 tablespoons apple cider vinegar

TOOLS & EQUIPMENT

Measuring cups/spoons
Knife
Large spoon
Cutting board
Box grater
Large bowl
Large pot with lid

1. **Cook the bacon.** Put the bacon in the large pot on the stove over medium heat. Cook the bacon for 8 to 10 minutes, until crisp. Carefully pour off most of the bacon fat, leaving 1 tablespoon in the pot.

2. **Cook the cabbage and apple.** Add the cabbage, apple, onion, and garlic to the pot and cook for 5 minutes, stirring occasionally.

3. **Season the cabbage.** Add the salt, pepper, honey, and hot water and cover with the lid. Turn the heat down to medium-low and cook for 10 minutes. Stir in the vinegar and cook for 2 more minutes, then serve.

Chicken and Sausage Gumbo · **PAGE** 73

CHAPTER
4

SOUPS AND SALADS

CURRIED SWEET POTATO SOUP

This is the perfect soup for fall and winter. It will warm you up and fill you up. Because it has no cream, it freezes well and will store frozen for a few months, so it's great for advance meal prep.

Dairy-Free, Gluten-Free, Leftover Friendly, Nut-Free, One Pot, Vegan

MAKES: *4 servings*
PREP TIME: *10 minutes*
COOK TIME: *30 minutes*

1 tablespoon olive oil

1 cup medium-diced onion

1 teaspoon minced
    fresh ginger

1 tablespoon minced garlic

¼ teaspoon red
    pepper flakes

2 tablespoons yellow
    curry powder

4 cups large-diced
    sweet potatoes

½ teaspoon kosher salt,
    or more as needed

¼ teaspoon black pepper,
    or more as needed

4 cups water, or more
    as needed

TOOLS & EQUIPMENT

Measuring cups/spoons
Knife
Wooden spoon
Cutting board
Large pot
Blender, immersion
    or countertop

1. **Heat a large pot over medium heat.** Add the olive oil.

2. **Cook the aromatics.** Add the onion to the pot and cook for 3 minutes, or until it softens. Add the ginger and garlic and cook for 1 minute. Add the red pepper flakes and curry powder and cook for 30 seconds.

3. **Cook the sweet potatoes.** Add the sweet potatoes, salt, pepper, and water. Bring to a boil, reduce the heat to low, and simmer for 20 minutes, or until the sweet potato is tender.

4. **Puree the soup.** Use the blender to puree the soup. Adjust the consistency of the soup by adding a little more water if needed. Taste the soup and add a bit more salt and pepper if it needs it.

HELPFUL HINT: When pureeing hot soup in a blender, always remove the center cover from the blender's lid, or open the lid's spout and cover it with a towel. This will prevent the pressure from building up in the blender jar, which can cause the top to blow off, sending hot soup everywhere.

SPICY PEANUT BUTTER SOUP

It may seem odd to put peanut butter in soup, but once you taste this, you will be a believer. This soup is a little sweet, a little spicy, a little nutty, and a lot delicious.

Dairy-Free, Gluten-Free, Leftover Friendly, One Pot, Vegan

MAKES: *4 servings*
PREP TIME: *15 minutes*
COOK TIME: *30 minutes*

1 tablespoon olive oil
1 cup medium-diced onion
2 tablespoons minced garlic
1 tablespoon minced fresh ginger
1 tablespoon yellow curry powder
1 tablespoon tomato paste
2 cups large-diced sweet potatoes
1 (15-ounce) can black beans, drained and rinsed
1 cup medium-diced green bell pepper
1 tablespoon brown sugar
2 tablespoons creamy peanut butter
½ teaspoon kosher salt, or more as needed
¼ teaspoon black pepper, or more as needed
4 cups water

TOOLS & EQUIPMENT

Measuring cups/spoons
Knife
Wooden spoon
Cutting board
Large pot

1. **Heat the large pot over medium-high heat.**

2. **Cook the aromatics and spices.** Add the olive oil and onion to the pot and cook for 3 minutes, or until the onion softens. Add the garlic and ginger and cook for 1 minute. Add the curry powder and cook for 30 seconds.

3. **Make the soup.** Add the tomato paste to the pot and cook, stirring with the wooden spoon, for 2 minutes. Add the sweet potatoes, black beans, green pepper, brown sugar, peanut butter, salt, pepper, and water and bring the pot to a boil. Turn the heat to low and simmer for 15 to 20 minutes, or until the sweet potatoes are tender.

4. **Adjust the seasoning.** Taste the soup and add salt and pepper as needed. Serve.

KICK IT UP A NOTCH: For an extra kick, add ¼ teaspoon cayenne along with the curry powder.

MEATBALL MINESTRONE

When you want a hearty soup that will fill you up, this minestrone is what you're looking for. It is a full meal in a bowl and the perfect portable lunch to take to work.

Dairy-Free, Gluten-Free, Leftover Friendly, Nut-Free, One Pot

MAKES: *6 servings*
PREP TIME: *10 minutes*
COOK TIME: *40 minutes*

2 tablespoons olive oil
1 cup small-diced onion
1 cup sliced carrots
¼ cup sliced celery
2 tablespoons minced garlic
½ teaspoon red
    pepper flakes
1 tablespoon dried
    Italian seasoning
1 (18-ounce) can
    tomato puree
2 cups medium-diced
    potatoes
8 cups water
1 (18-ounce) can white
    beans, drained and rinsed
1 recipe meatballs from
    Meatballs with Onion
    Gravy (page 118),
    without gravy

TOOLS & EQUIPMENT

Measuring cups/spoons
Knife
Wooden spoon
Cutting board
Large pot

1. **Cook the vegetables.** Heat the large pot over medium-high heat. Add the olive oil, onion, carrots, and celery. Cook for 5 minutes, then add the garlic and cook for 1 more minute.

2. **Add the rest of the ingredients.** Add the red pepper flakes, Italian seasoning, tomato puree, diced potatoes, water, and beans to the pot. Bring to a boil, then reduce the heat to medium-low and simmer for 20 minutes, or until the potatoes are cooked.

3. **Finish and serve.** Add the meatballs to the soup, stir with the wooden spoon, and heat for 10 minutes to warm them through. Serve in large bowls.

TAKE THE EASY WAY OUT: To make this soup a little easier, you can substitute Italian sausage for the meatballs. Either use previously cooked sausage or roast the sausage in the oven at 400°F for 20 minutes and let cool for 10 minutes; slice and add to the soup at the end.

CHICKEN AND SAUSAGE GUMBO

The secret to a good gumbo is getting the roux right. A *roux* is a mixture containing equal quantities of flour and fat, usually butter, which is cooked together, then used to thicken a soup or sauce. The flavor of gumbo largely comes from the roux.

Leftover Friendly, Nut-Free, One Pot

MAKES: *4 servings*
PREP TIME: *15 minutes*
COOK TIME: *35 minutes*

2 tablespoons olive oil, divided
8 ounces skinless, boneless chicken thighs, diced
1 tablespoon butter
½ cup small-diced onion
½ cup small-diced celery
½ cup small-diced green bell pepper
½ cup small-diced red bell pepper
1 tablespoon minced garlic
1 tablespoon Cajun seasoning
2 tablespoons all-purpose flour
8 ounces smoked sausage, sliced ½ inch thick
4 cups water or chicken broth
½ teaspoon kosher salt, or more as needed
¼ teaspoon black pepper, or more as needed

TOOLS & EQUIPMENT

Measuring cups/spoons
Knife
Wooden spoon
Cutting board
Large pot

1. **Cook the chicken thighs.** Heat the large pot over medium-high heat. Add 1 tablespoon of olive oil and the chicken thighs. Cook for 7 to 8 minutes, or until the chicken is no longer pink, stirring once or twice. Take the chicken out of the pot and set it aside.

2. **Cook the vegetables.** Add the remaining 1 tablespoon of olive oil to the pot along with the butter, onion, celery, and bell peppers. Cook for 6 to 7 minutes, or until the celery and onion soften. Add the garlic and Cajun seasoning and cook for 1 minute.

3. **Make a roux.** Sprinkle the flour over the vegetables and stir for 4 minutes. This makes the roux that will thicken the gumbo.

4. **Add the remaining ingredients and simmer.** Put the chicken back in the pot along with the sausage, water, salt, and pepper. Bring to a boil, then reduce the heat to low and simmer for 15 minutes, or until the soup coats the back of a spoon.

5. **Adjust the seasoning.** Taste the soup and add salt and pepper as needed. Serve.

KICK IT UP A NOTCH: Cook 8 ounces shrimp with the chicken to make a true gumbo.

CREAM OF MUSHROOM SOUP

Cream of mushroom soup isn't just something an elderly relative uses as a sauce for pork chops. It is very much its own thing, and it is delicious when done right. Avoid the canned stuff because now you can make your own. And yes, you can use this soup as a sauce for pork chops, too.

Leftover Friendly, Nut-Free, One Pot, Vegetarian

MAKES: *4 servings*
PREP TIME: *15 minutes*
COOK TIME: *25 minutes*

1 tablespoon olive oil
1 tablespoon butter
1 cup small-diced onion
1 tablespoon minced garlic
1 pound sliced cremini mushrooms
2 tablespoons all-purpose flour
¼ cup dry white wine
2 cups water or vegetable broth
2 teaspoons chopped fresh rosemary
½ teaspoon kosher salt, or more as needed
⅛ teaspoon black pepper, or more as needed
½ cup heavy cream

TOOLS & EQUIPMENT

Measuring spoons
Measuring cups
Knife
Cutting board
Large pot

1. **Cook the mushrooms.** Put the large pot over medium-high heat. Add the olive oil and butter. When the butter starts to foam, add the onion, garlic, and mushrooms. Cook for 5 minutes. Sprinkle the flour over the mushrooms and stir for 2 minutes.

2. **Add the seasoning.** Pour the wine into the pot, cook for 1 minute, then add the water, rosemary, salt, and pepper. Bring the pot to a boil, then reduce the heat to low and simmer for 15 minutes, or until the soup is thick enough to coat the back of a spoon.

3. **Add the cream, heat, and serve.** Pour the cream into the pot and cook just until it is hot. Taste the soup and add more salt and pepper as needed.

KICK IT UP A NOTCH: Use a couple varieties of mushrooms to add extra flavor. Puree the soup to make it a little more elegant.

LENTIL AND BLACK BEAN SOUP

If you are looking for a protein boost but aren't in the mood for meat, this lentil and black bean soup has you covered. It's the perfect thing to make, freeze, and then heat up when you need a quick meal.

Dairy-Free, Gluten-Free, Leftover Friendly, Nut-Free, One Pot, Vegan

MAKES: *4 servings*
PREP TIME: *10 minutes*
COOK TIME: *30 minutes*

1 tablespoon olive oil
1 cup small-diced onion
½ cup small-diced celery
½ cup small-diced carrot
1 tablespoon minced garlic
1 tablespoon yellow
    curry powder
2 tablespoons tomato paste
½ cup dried red
    lentils, rinsed
1 (15-ounce) can black
    beans, rinsed and drained
4 cups vegetable
    broth or water
½ teaspoon kosher salt,
    or more as needed
¼ teaspoon black pepper,
    or more as needed

TOOLS & EQUIPMENT

Measuring spoons
Measuring cups
Knife
Cutting board
Large pot

1. **Cook the flavor base.** Heat the large pot over medium-high heat. Add the olive oil, onion, celery, and carrot and cook for 5 minutes. Add the garlic and cook for 1 minute more, then add the curry powder and tomato paste and cook for another minute.

2. **Cook the beans.** Add the lentils, black beans, broth, salt, and pepper to the pot and bring the liquid to a boil. Reduce the heat to medium-low and simmer for 20 minutes, or until the lentils are tender. Taste, and season with additional salt and pepper if needed. Serve.

CLASSIC SEAFOOD CHOWDER

A good seafood chowder is creamy but not heavy. It is thick but not gloopy. And it tastes of fresh seafood but isn't fishy. This chowder checks all those boxes and is an impressive recipe for a potluck or dinner party.

Leftover Friendly, Nut-Free, One Pot

MAKES: *6 servings*
PREP TIME: *20 minutes*
COOK TIME: *30 minutes*

1 tablespoon olive oil
2 tablespoons butter
1 cup small-diced onion
½ cup small-diced celery
½ cup small-diced carrot
3 tablespoons
    all-purpose flour
4 cups water or chicken broth
2 cups medium-diced
    potatoes
1 teaspoon kosher salt,
    or more as needed
¼ teaspoon black pepper,
    or more as needed
8 ounces shrimp (any size),
    peeled and medium-diced
8 ounces bay scallops
    or medium-diced
    sea scallops
2 cups heavy cream
1 pound white fish fillet,
    medium-diced

TOOLS & EQUIPMENT

Measuring cups/spoons
Knife
Cutting board
Large pot

1. **Cook the flavor base.** Put the large pot on the stove over medium-high heat. Add the olive oil and butter. When the butter melts and starts to foam, add the onion, celery, and carrot and cook for 5 to 7 minutes, or until the onion and celery soften. Add the flour to the pot and cook, stirring with the wooden spoon, for 2 minutes.

2. **Cook the potatoes.** Pour the water into the pot and stir to blend with the vegetable mixture. Add the potatoes, salt, and pepper. Bring to a boil, turn the heat down to medium, and cook for 10 minutes, or until the potatoes are tender.

3. **Make the chowder.** Add the shrimp and scallops to the pot and cook for 3 minutes. Add the cream and heat for 2 to 3 minutes, or until the chowder is heated through. Gently stir to make sure nothing is sticking to the bottom of the pot, then add the fish. Cook for 3 to 4 minutes, until fully cooked.

4. **Taste and serve.** Taste the chowder, season it with salt and pepper if needed, and serve.

KALE SUPER SALAD

Kale used to be just a green that was put on the side of a plate as garnish. Almost no one ever ate it. Suddenly, it's everywhere and everyone is eating it. Now you can, too. The secret to making kale palatable is to massage oil and lemon juice into it, then let it sit for a few minutes.

30 Minutes, Dairy-Free, Gluten-Free, Vegetarian

MAKES: *4 servings*

PREP TIME: *20 minutes*

1 bunch fresh kale, washed, dried, and stemmed

1 tablespoon olive oil

2 teaspoons fresh lemon juice

2 tablespoons apple cider vinegar

1 teaspoon Dijon mustard

2 teaspoons honey

½ teaspoon kosher salt

⅛ teaspoon black pepper

¼ cup grapeseed oil

1 green apple, cored

¼ cup dried cranberries

¼ cup sliced almonds

¼ cup sunflower seeds

TOOLS & EQUIPMENT

Measuring cups/spoons

Knife

Whisk

Cutting board

Large bowl

Small bowl

1. **Massage the kale.** Cut or tear the kale into bite-size pieces (no bigger than 1 inch square) and put in the large bowl. Add the olive oil and lemon juice, and use your fingers to massage the oil and juice into the kale for 3 to 4 minutes. Let the kale sit for 10 minutes.

2. **Make the dressing.** In the small bowl, whisk together the vinegar, mustard, honey, salt, and pepper. While whisking, slowly pour in the grapeseed oil a few drops at a time. Continue until all the oil has been incorporated.

3. **Assemble the salad.** Cut the apple in half, then cut it into ⅛-inch-thick slices and add it to the kale. Stir in the cranberries, almonds, and sunflower seeds, top with the dressing, toss well, and serve.

TAKE THE EASY WAY OUT: Use a store-bought cider or balsamic dressing instead of making your own.

Roasted Vegetable and Halloumi Salad

Halloumi is a firm Greek goat/sheep's milk cheese that holds its shape when cooked. Its firmness makes this cheese perfect for searing in a pan or on a grill, and it's best when cooked with olive oil and finished with a little lemon juice. Halloumi is a "squeaky cheese," meaning that when you eat it, it squeaks against your teeth. That explains why I was originally going to call this salad "The Squeaker," but who wants to eat that?

5 Ingredients, 30 Minutes, Gluten-Free, Nut-Free, Vegetarian

MAKES: *4 servings*

PREP TIME: *45 minutes*

COOK TIME: *5 minutes*

2 cups fresh arugula

1 recipe Italian Roasted Vegetables (page 59)

2 tablespoons olive oil, divided

1 tablespoon balsamic vinegar

8 ounces halloumi cheese

Juice of ½ lemon

TOOLS & EQUIPMENT

Measuring spoons

Measuring cups

Large spoon

Large bowl

Medium nonstick skillet

1. **Assemble the salad.** Mix the arugula and roasted vegetables in the large bowl with 1 tablespoon of olive oil and the balsamic vinegar. Divide the mixture among 4 plates.

2. **Slice and cook the halloumi.** Cut the halloumi into ¼-inch-thick slices. Heat the nonstick skillet over medium-high heat. Add the remaining 1 tablespoon of olive oil, then the halloumi. Cook the halloumi for 2 to 3 minutes per side, or until the cheese browns. Squeeze the lemon juice over the cheese.

3. **Add the halloumi to the salad.** Divide the halloumi among the 4 salads. Spoon the pan juices over the salad and serve.

GREEK-STYLE PASTA SALAD

We've all been to potlucks or community gatherings where someone has brought a pasta salad that was pretty much just pasta with a ketchup and mayonnaise dressing. Is there anything wrong with that? Of course not. But why not dress to impress? Your pasta salad, that is. This Greek pasta salad has everything you love in a Greek salad, but with pasta in it as well. I say "Yamas!" to that.

Gluten-Free, Leftover Friendly, Nut-Free, Vegetarian

MAKES: *6 servings*
PREP TIME: *15 minutes, plus 1 hour to chill*
COOK TIME: *15 minutes*

1 teaspoon kosher salt
2 cups penne
1 cup small-diced green bell pepper
¼ cup small-diced red onion
1 cup small-diced cucumber
12 grape tomatoes, halved
½ cup sliced Kalamata olives
½ cup store-bought Greek salad dressing
½ cup crumbled feta cheese

TOOLS & EQUIPMENT

Measuring cups/spoons
Knife
Cutting board
Colander
Large bowl
Large pot
Plastic wrap

1. **Cook the pasta.** Fill the large pot three-fourths full of hot water. Add the salt and bring to a boil over high heat. Add the pasta and cook according to the package directions, about 10 minutes, until tender. Drain the pasta in the colander and rinse under cold water until cool to the touch.

2. **Combine the ingredients.** While the pasta is cooking, mix the green pepper, red onion, cucumber, grape tomatoes, olives, and dressing in the large bowl.

3. **Assemble the salad.** Add the cooled pasta to the salad and toss to coat with the dressing.

4. **Chill the salad.** Top the salad with the crumbled feta, cover the bowl with plastic wrap, and put it in the fridge to chill for 1 hour before serving.

SUPERSIZE IT: You can easily double this recipe, which makes it great for a potluck, dinner party, or barbecue.

CITRUS SALAD WITH ARUGULA AND ALMONDS

This is the perfect salad for when you have a few people coming over and want to wow them. It's the kind of salad you make for your parents, and they're like, "Oh, damn. We did a good job. Our kid is doing better than we thought."

30 Minutes, Gluten-Free, One Pot

MAKES: *4 servings*

PREP TIME: *15 minutes*

2 tablespoons red wine vinegar

2 teaspoons mustard of choice

2 teaspoons honey

¼ teaspoon kosher salt

⅛ teaspoon black pepper

¼ cup olive oil

1 navel orange

1 blood orange

3 cups fresh arugula

4 slices prosciutto

¼ cup sliced almonds

¼ cup grated Parmesan cheese

TOOLS & EQUIPMENT

Measuring cups/spoons

Knife

Whisk

Cheese grater

Cutting board

Medium bowl

1. **Make the dressing.** In the medium bowl, combine the vinegar, mustard, honey, salt, and pepper. While whisking, slowly pour in the olive oil. Whisk until all the oil has been incorporated.

2. **Prep the oranges.** Peel the oranges. Divide the segments of the navel orange and add them to the bowl. Slice the blood orange across the segments into ⅛-inch slices, then put them in the bowl as well.

3. **Add the arugula and dressing.** Add the arugula and dressing to the bowl and stir. Ensure that all the arugula is coated with the dressing.

4. **Assemble the salad.** Transfer the arugula salad to 4 serving plates. Cut the prosciutto slices into 4 strips each, and place them around the salads. Top with the almonds and a sprinkling of Parmesan, then serve.

Sesame-Ginger Green Bean Salad

Who knew that green beans could be so delicious? Seriously. This is a super-simple salad that is packed with flavor. It's flavorful when fresh, but it is even better the next day, after the green beans have had time to absorb some of the dressing.

30 Minutes, Dairy-Free, Leftover Friendly, Nut-Free, Vegetarian

MAKES: *4 servings*
PREP TIME: *20 minutes*
COOK TIME: *5 minutes*

2 pounds fresh green beans
1 teaspoon salt
2 tablespoons soy sauce
1 tablespoon honey
2 tablespoons rice vinegar
2 teaspoons grated
    fresh ginger
1 teaspoon grated garlic
½ teaspoon red
    pepper flakes
1 tablespoon sesame seeds
¼ cup grapeseed oil
1 tablespoon toasted
    sesame oil

TOOLS & EQUIPMENT

Measuring cups/spoons
Whisk
Grater
Colander
Large bowl
Large pot

1. **Prep the green beans.** Cut the tips and any remaining stem pieces from the green beans.

2. **Cook the beans.** Fill the large pot three-fourths full of water. Add the salt and bring to a boil over high heat. Add the beans and bring the water back to a boil. Boil the beans for 2 minutes. Pour the green beans into the colander, then rinse under cold water until they are cool to the touch.

3. **Make the dressing.** In the large bowl, whisk together the soy sauce, honey, rice vinegar, ginger, garlic, red pepper flakes, and sesame seeds. While whisking, pour the grapeseed oil into the bowl in a slow, steady stream until it is all incorporated. Slowly add the sesame oil and stir again.

4. **Assemble the salad.** Add the green beans to the dressing, let them sit for 10 minutes, and then serve.

TAKE THE EASY WAY OUT: Use a store-bought sesame-ginger dressing.

Chicken and Bacon Waldorf Salad

The Waldorf salad is a classic mixture of fruit and nuts mixed with mayonnaise and served on lettuce leaves. It is a throwback to a simpler time, whatever that means. This version stays pretty true to the original, with the noted addition of roasted chicken.

Dairy-Free, Gluten-Free

MAKES: *2 servings*
PREP TIME: *15 minutes*
COOK TIME: *25 minutes*

2 teaspoons olive oil
2 (5-ounce) skinless, boneless chicken breasts
½ teaspoon salt
⅛ teaspoon black pepper
½ cup medium-diced cucumber
½ cup medium-diced green apple
¼ cup medium-diced celery
½ cup green grapes, halved
¼ cup pecans
¼ cup mayonnaise
4 leaves iceberg lettuce

TOOLS & EQUIPMENT

Measuring spoons
Measuring cups
Knife
Cutting board
Instant-read thermometer
Large bowl
Small roasting pan

1. **Preheat your oven to 400°F.**

2. **Roast the chicken breasts.** Pour the olive oil into the small roasting pan. Add the chicken breasts and roll them around to coat them in the oil. Season the chicken with the salt and pepper, then roast for about 25 minutes, or until the chicken's internal temperature reaches 165°F.

3. **Combine the remaining salad ingredients.** In the large bowl, combine the cucumber, apple, celery, grapes, pecans, and mayonnaise. Mix well.

4. **Assemble the salads and serve.** Place the lettuce leaves on 2 serving plates and fill them with the salad. Slice the chicken breasts and arrange them on top. Serve.

TAKE THE EASY WAY OUT: Use leftover rotisserie or roast chicken instead of cooking the breasts.

CLASSIC POTATO SALAD

Potato salad is just as common at a backyard barbecue as the grill itself. But why wait for your next invite to have a delicious potato salad? Make this classic recipe for yourself whenever you want.

Dairy-Free, Gluten-Free, Leftover Friendly, Nut-Free, Vegetarian

MAKES: *4 servings*
PREP TIME: *20 minutes, plus overnight to chill*
COOK TIME: *30 minutes*

1 pound yellow-fleshed baby potatoes

2 large eggs

½ cup mayonnaise

1 tablespoon mustard of choice

1 tablespoon distilled white vinegar

2 teaspoons sugar

¼ teaspoon paprika

¼ teaspoon salt

⅛ teaspoon black pepper

1 teaspoon dried dill

2 tablespoons relish of choice

1. **Cook the potatoes.** Put the potatoes in the large pot and cover with water. Bring to a boil and cook until the potatoes are tender, about 20 minutes. Drain the potatoes in the colander, then put them in the fridge to cool completely. This will take a minimum of 2 hours. (It's best to cook the potatoes the day before and chill them overnight.)

2. **Hard-boil the eggs.** Put the eggs in the medium pot and cover with water. Bring to a boil over high heat, then reduce the heat to medium. Cook the eggs for 7 minutes. Using the small strainer, drain the water off the eggs. Gently crack the shells with a spoon, and run the eggs under cold water until completely cool. Peel the eggs and keep them in the fridge until you are ready to use them.

3. **Combine the remaining ingredients.** In the large bowl, combine the mayonnaise, mustard, vinegar, sugar, paprika, salt, pepper, dill, and relish.

4. **Assemble the salad.** Cut the cooled potatoes into quarters and add to the bowl. Cut the eggs into ⅛-inch slices and add to the bowl. Mix gently, then serve.

TOOLS & EQUIPMENT

Measuring spoons

Measuring cups

Small strainer

Colander

Large bowl

Medium pot

Large pot

HACK IT 5 WAYS

The great thing about potato salad is that it is easy to jazz up. Here are five small changes you can make to your potato salad to make it shine:

(1) Add crispy bacon bits to it. Obviously.

(2) Add 1 or 2 teaspoons of prepared horse-radish to the mayo.

(3) Add 1 tablespoon of chopped chives or scallions to the salad.

(4) Add ¼ cup cooked peas and ¼ cup crispy prosciutto to the salad.

(5) Add ¼ cup grated Cheddar cheese and ¼ cup crispy bacon, and switch the dressing to ranch.

PIZZA SALAD

You know when you're in the shower and weird questions pop into your head? Well, this salad is the answer to the question, "Why can't a pizza be a salad?" My friend, a pizza can be a salad, and you don't even have to get it delivered.

30 Minutes, Nut-Free

MAKES: *2 servings*
PREP TIME: *15 minutes*
COOK TIME: *15 minutes*

4 tablespoons olive oil, divided

½ cup torn 1-inch pieces sourdough bread

½ cup medium-diced red bell pepper

½ cup medium-diced red onion

12 grape tomatoes

½ cup small-diced pepperoni

2 teaspoons dried Italian seasoning

2 cups fresh arugula

¼ cup grated mozzarella cheese

TOOLS & EQUIPMENT

Measuring cups/spoons
Knife
Wooden spoon
Medium skillet
Wooden spoon
Cheese grater
Large bowl

1. **Toast the bread.** Heat the medium skillet over medium-high heat. Add 1 tablespoon of olive oil and the bread pieces. Cook, stirring every minute or so, for 4 minutes, or until the bread is toasted on all sides. Take the bread out of the pan and set aside. Put the skillet back on the heat.

2. **Cook the vegetables and pepperoni.** Add the remaining 3 tablespoons of olive oil to the skillet along with the bell pepper, red onion, tomatoes, and pepperoni. Cook for 7 to 8 minutes, or until the pepper and onion are soft. Add the Italian seasoning and cook for 2 more minutes.

3. **Toss the salad.** Put the arugula in the large bowl and add the mixture from the skillet. Toss together, then spread on a serving platter. Top with the croutons and sprinkle with the mozzarella. Serve. Mic drop optional.

Pan-Fried Haddock Burger · PAGE 104

CHAPTER 5

MEALS FOR ONE

THE PERFECT PAN-SEARED STRIP STEAK

As our earliest ancestors used to say, "Steak good." We've come a long way from those wacky cave-dwelling cousins of ours, but one thing remains true: Steak is good. The instructions here will give you a perfect medium-rare. If you like your steak a little rarer, cook it for 30 seconds less per side. For a little more well-done, cook it for 30 seconds more per side. For a pop of color, top with a few thyme sprigs before serving.

5 Ingredients, Gluten-Free, Leftover Friendly, Nut-Free, One Pot

MAKES: *1 serving*
PREP TIME: *30 minutes*
COOK TIME: *10 minutes*

---

1 (6-ounce) New
   York strip steak

½ teaspoon kosher salt

¼ teaspoon black pepper

2 teaspoons canola oil

2 tablespoons butter

2 garlic cloves, peeled
   and crushed

TOOLS & EQUIPMENT

Measuring spoons

Measuring cups

Tongs

Large spoon

Medium skillet

Cutting board

1. **Prep the steak.** Take the steak out of the fridge and leave it on your counter in its original packaging for 30 minutes to come to room temperature. This will help it cook more evenly. Then, season the steak on both sides with the salt and pepper.

2. **Warm the skillet.** Put the medium skillet on the stove over medium-high heat, and leave it alone for 3 to 4 minutes to get hot.

3. **Cook the steak.** Pour the canola oil into the skillet, add the steak, and cook without touching it for 2 minutes. Flip the steak with tongs, add the butter and garlic to the pan, and use a spoon to continuously scoop the melted butter onto the steak for 2 minutes.

4. **Rest the steak.** Take the steak out of the pan and set it on the cutting board. Let it rest for 5 minutes before slicing it. Serve the steak topped with some of the butter from the pan.

KICK IT UP A NOTCH: After the steak comes out of the skillet, add 2 tablespoons minced onion to the skillet, cook for 1 minute, add 2 ounces (¼ cup) good whiskey, cook for 2 minutes, and then add 1 tablespoon heavy cream. Bring the cream to a boil, taste, and adjust the seasoning with salt and pepper, then pour the sauce over your steak.

LEMON AND GARLIC SCALLOP PASTA

If you like scallops, garlic, and lemon, you're going to love this pasta. It is bursting with flavor, and it's easy to make. Plus, it comes together in just 20 minutes. You can't go wrong with that.

30 Minutes, Nut-Free

MAKES: *1 serving*
PREP TIME: *5 minutes*
COOK TIME: *15 minutes*

3½ ounces fettuccine

1 tablespoon olive oil

2 tablespoons butter

5 ounces sea or bay scallops

1 tablespoon sliced garlic

¼ teaspoon kosher salt

⅛ teaspoon black pepper

¼ teaspoon red
    pepper flakes

1 lemon

2 tablespoons grated
    Parmesan cheese

TOOLS & EQUIPMENT

Measuring spoons

Knife

Wooden spoon

Cheese grater

Cutting board

Colander

Large pot

Medium nonstick skillet

1. **Cook the pasta.** Fill the large pot with water and bring to a boil. Add the pasta and cook according to the package instructions, 8 to 10 minutes, until al dente. Drain in a colander.

2. **Cook the scallops.** Heat the medium nonstick skillet over medium-high heat and add the olive oil and butter. When the butter melts and starts to foam, add the scallops, garlic, salt, and pepper. Cook for 2 minutes, stirring occasionally with the wooden spoon. Add the red pepper flakes and cook, stirring, for 1 minute.

3. **Add the pasta to the skillet.** Add the pasta to the skillet, stir to mix with the scallops, and heat for 1 minute.

4. **Finish the dish.** Squeeze the lemon juice into the pan and cook for 30 seconds. Take the pan off the heat, sprinkle on the Parmesan, and serve.

HELPFUL HINT: If you really want to step up your pasta game, there are two things you should always add to your pasta dishes right before you serve them. One is a tablespoon or two of chopped fresh parsley, and the other is a tablespoon or two of butter. Seriously, every pasta dish. Try it.

DOUBLE-STACK SMASH BURGER

This burger was made for late-night cravings. You know the ones. You just have to have a burger, but you don't want to leave the house. Luckily, this burger will satisfy any time that craving hits you.

30 Minutes, Nut-Free

MAKES: *1 serving*
PREP TIME: *10 minutes*
COOK TIME: *10 minutes*

6 ounces ground beef

¼ teaspoon kosher salt

⅛ teaspoon black pepper

1 teaspoon minced garlic

2 teaspoons canola oil

½ cup thinly sliced onion

2 slices Cheddar cheese

1 burger bun

Condiments of choice, for topping

TOOLS & EQUIPMENT

Measuring spoons

Measuring cups

Knife

Spatula

Medium bowl

Medium skillet with lid

Toaster

Parchment paper

1. **Make the burgers.** In the medium bowl, combine the beef, salt, pepper, and garlic. Mix well. Divide the meat mixture in half and roll each half into a ball.

2. **Heat the medium skillet over medium-high heat.** Add the canola oil to the skillet and allow to get hot.

3. **Cook the onion and burgers.** Divide the onion slices into 2 piles and place them in the skillet about 2 inches apart. Put a meatball on top of each onion stack. Lay a piece of parchment paper over the meatballs and press down with a spatula to flatten them. Discard the parchment paper. Cook the burgers for 2 minutes, then flip with the spatula and cook for 2 more minutes.

4. **Top the burgers.** Put a slice of cheese on each burger, put the lid on the skillet, turn the heat down to medium-low, and cook for 1 more minute or until the cheese melts.

5. **Toast the bun and serve.** Toast the bun in your toaster on the bagel setting, if it has one. Stack the burgers on the bun's bottom half and slather with your favorite condiments, then add the bun top and enjoy.

KICK IT UP A NOTCH: Mix 2 tablespoons mayonnaise with 1 to 2 teaspoons prepared horseradish, and spread that on the bun. Delicious.

CHICKEN FAJITA SKILLET

Serve this dish with a warm tortilla, and you have a fajita. Serve it over rice, and you have . . . okay, maybe it won't have a cool name if you serve it over rice, but it will still taste good. You can even crack an egg or two on top of it, finish it in a 350°F oven for 10 minutes, and you've got breakfast.

30 Minutes, Gluten-Free, Leftover Friendly, Nut-Free, One Pot

MAKES: *1 serving*
PREP TIME: *10 minutes*
COOK TIME: *10 minutes*

1 tablespoon olive oil

1 (5-ounce) skinless, boneless chicken breast, cut into thin slices

1½ teaspoons Cajun seasoning

¼ teaspoon salt

¼ cup small-diced onion

½ cup small-diced green bell pepper

½ cup small-diced red bell pepper

¼ cup grated Cheddar cheese

TOOLS & EQUIPMENT

Measuring cups/spoons

Knife

Wooden spoon

Cheese grater

Cutting board

Medium nonstick skillet

1. **Heat the pan.** Place the medium nonstick skillet over medium-high heat, allow it to warm, and then add the olive oil.

2. **Cook the chicken.** Add the chicken, Cajun seasoning, and salt to the pan and cook for 4 minutes.

3. **Cook the veggies.** Add the onion and red and green bell peppers to the pan and cook for 3 more minutes.

4. **Top with the cheese.** Take the skillet off the heat, sprinkle with the cheese, and serve.

KICK IT UP A NOTCH: Top the skillet mix with salsa and sour cream for a more authentic fajita taste. You can also add ¼ cup black beans and 1 tablespoon minced jalapeño when cooking the peppers and onion for a little more substance and heat.

FLATBREAD PIZZA

Making pizza at home doesn't have to be hard. Using a flatbread like naan means you don't have to put in the effort to make the dough. It also means that the pizza crust will cook much quicker than a traditional dough crust. This recipe uses salami, jarred roasted red peppers, and pickled banana peppers, and it is fantastic.

30 Minutes, Leftover Friendly, Nut-Free

MAKES: *1 serving*
PREP TIME: *10 minutes*
COOK TIME: *15 minutes*

¼ cup tomato puree

1 teaspoon Italian seasoning

½ teaspoon sugar

¼ teaspoon kosher salt

⅛ teaspoon black pepper

2 tablespoons olive oil

1 (6-inch) flatbread, such as naan

4 tablespoons grated mozzarella cheese, divided

4 slices salami

2 tablespoons sliced roasted red pepper

1 tablespoon chopped hot pickled banana pepper

TOOLS & EQUIPMENT

Measuring cups/spoons

Knife

Wooden spoon

Cheese grater

Cutting board

Small bowl

Sheet pan

1. **Preheat your oven to 400°F.**

2. **Make the sauce.** In the small bowl, combine the tomato puree, Italian seasoning, sugar, salt, and pepper; mix well.

3. **Assemble the pizza.** Spread the olive oil out in the sheet pan and put the flatbread on it. Spread the sauce on the flatbread, then top with 2 tablespoons of mozzarella, the salami, roasted red pepper, and banana pepper. Sprinkle on the remaining 2 tablespoons of mozzarella.

4. **Bake the pizza.** Put the sheet pan in the oven and bake for 12 to 15 minutes, or until the bread is golden brown and the cheese has melted.

5. **Cool and serve.** Let the pizza cool for 2 to 3 minutes, cut into quarters, and enjoy.

Chicken Banh Mi Burger

The banh mi is a Vietnamese sandwich most often made with roasted pork, pâté, pickled vegetables, cilantro, and cucumber on a small baguette. This version replaces the pork with chicken, the pâté with Sriracha and mayonnaise, and the baguette with a burger bun, all without compromising taste. This sandwich hits the spot for one person, but it is easy to make for many. Think about preparing this the next time you get invited to a backyard barbecue.

Dairy-Free, Nut-Free, One Pot

MAKES: *1 serving*
PREP TIME: *10 minutes, plus overnight to marinate*
COOK TIME: *20 minutes*

1 tablespoon honey

1 tablespoon soy sauce

2 teaspoons Sriracha, divided

2 teaspoons sliced garlic

1 teaspoon sliced fresh ginger

1 skinless, boneless chicken breast

Canola oil, for coating the rack

1 burger bun

1 tablespoon mayonnaise

4 (⅛-inch) slices cucumber

12 fresh cilantro leaves

5 or 6 slices pickled banana pepper

1. **Make the marinade.** In a medium zippered plastic bag, combine the honey, soy sauce, 1 teaspoon of Sriracha, garlic, and ginger.

2. **Marinate the chicken.** Lay the chicken breast flat on your cutting board and slice it horizontally through the middle into 2 cutlets. Put the chicken slices in the bag with the marinade. Gently squeeze the air out of the bag, seal it, and put it in the fridge overnight.

3. **Preheat your oven to 400°F.** Line the broiler pan with aluminum foil and put the rack in place. Brush the rack with a light coating of canola oil.

4. **Cook the chicken.** Put the marinated chicken on the broiler rack and roast for 15 minutes. Flip the chicken and roast for another 5 minutes. Take the chicken out of the oven.

Measuring spoons

Knife

Cutting board

Medium zippered plastic bag

Toaster

Broiler pan with rack

Aluminum foil

5. **Toast the bun and make the sandwich.** Toast the burger bun in the toaster or in the oven for 4 to 5 minutes. Spread the mayonnaise on the top and bottom of the bun, then add the remaining 1 teaspoon of Sriracha. Put the chicken on the bottom half, and top with the cucumber, cilantro, and banana pepper. Add the bun top and serve.

SUPERSIZE IT: You can easily multiply the marinade ingredients and marinate as much chicken as you like. You can roast the chicken in the oven, according to the recipe, or grill it for 10 to 12 minutes.

Stir-Fried Noodles

The beauty of stir-fried noodles is that they can be whatever you want them to be. The key is to use all fresh ingredients to get the most flavor. For the vegetables, a combination of carrots, onion, and celery will work just as well as a combination of bean sprouts, snow peas, and red bell pepper. Make this your own and it will quickly become one of your go-to meals.

30 Minutes, Dairy-Free, Leftover Friendly, Nut-Free

MAKES: *1 serving*
PREP TIME: *15 minutes*
COOK TIME: *10 minutes*

2 ounces dried rice noodles

1 tablespoon canola oil

½ cup medium-diced raw protein (chicken thighs, pork, beef, scallops, or shrimp)

1 tablespoon minced garlic

1 cup thinly sliced vegetables (see headnote)

1 tablespoon brown sugar

2 tablespoons soy sauce

TOOLS & EQUIPMENT

Measuring cups/spoons

Knife

Wooden spoon

Cutting board

Colander

Medium bowl

Large nonstick skillet

1. **Soak the noodles.** Put the dried noodles in the medium bowl and pour boiling water over them. Press the noodles down to make sure they are submerged and soak them for 7 to 8 minutes, or until they are soft. Stir them every 2 minutes to ensure all the noodles are soaking evenly. When the noodles are soft, drain them and rinse them in the colander under cold water.

2. **Heat the large nonstick skillet over medium-high heat.**

3. **Cook the protein and vegetables.** Heat the canola oil and protein of choice in the hot skillet and cook until it browns, about 5 minutes. Add the garlic and cook for 30 seconds. Then add the vegetables and cook for 2 minutes, stirring with the wooden spoon.

4. **Combine with noodles.** Stir in the noodles, then add the brown sugar and soy sauce, cook for 2 more minutes, and serve.

HELPFUL HINT: If you've made a stir-fry of any kind and have noticed that some liquid pools in the bottom of the pan, one of two things has happened. Either the pan wasn't hot enough when you started cooking or you added too many ingredients at once and cooled the pan down. Prevent this by making sure your pan is hot and by adding ingredients in stages rather than all at once.

COCONUT CURRY SHRIMP

Thanks to Forrest Gump, we all know about 500 ways to cook shrimp, but here is one Bubba didn't mention. These coconut curry shrimp are delish over rice or pasta, or served as an appetizer. You can find Thai red curry paste in most grocery stores, and it packs a punch of flavor. This recipe also works with scallops, haddock, or even chicken wings.

30 Minutes, Dairy-Free, Gluten-Free, One Pot

MAKES: *1 serving*
PREP TIME: *5 minutes*
COOK TIME: *10 minutes*

2 teaspoons canola oil

6 ounces shrimp, peeled

1 teaspoon minced fresh ginger

1 teaspoon minced garlic

2 teaspoons Thai red curry paste

¼ teaspoon kosher salt

⅓ cup coconut milk

½ lime

1 tablespoon chopped fresh cilantro

TOOLS & EQUIPMENT

Measuring cups/spoons

Knife

Wooden spoon

Spatula

Cutting board

Medium skillet

1. **Cook the shrimp and aromatics.** Heat the medium skillet over medium-high heat. Add the canola oil and shrimp, cook for 1 minute, and then flip and cook for another minute. Add the ginger and garlic and cook for 1 more minute.

2. **Cook the curry.** Add the curry paste and salt and cook for 1 minute. Add the coconut milk and cook, stirring with the wooden spoon, for 2 minutes.

3. **Finish and serve.** Take the skillet off the heat and squeeze the juice from the lime over it. Sprinkle with the cilantro and serve.

HELPFUL HINT: Cooking the curry paste for a minute before adding the coconut milk helps intensify its flavor. Don't worry if it sticks to the pan. It will release when you pour in the coconut milk.

GINGER BEEF LETTUCE WRAPS

Lettuce wraps are a quick, light meal that you can make with ground beef, pork, chicken, or turkey. Serve them with steamed rice and fresh vegetables like julienned carrots and sliced cucumber to round out the meal a little bit. Chinese five-spice powder is a spice blend that you can find in most grocery stores; it goes especially well with beef, pork, and duck.

30 Minutes, Dairy-Free, Leftover Friendly, Nut-Free, One Pot

MAKES: *1 serving*
PREP TIME: *10 minutes*
COOK TIME: *10 minutes*

2 teaspoons canola oil

6 ounces lean ground beef

1 teaspoon minced garlic

1 tablespoon minced fresh ginger

2 scallions (green and white parts), sliced

¼ teaspoon kosher salt

1 teaspoon five-spice powder

1 teaspoon Sriracha

1 teaspoon soy sauce

1 teaspoon honey

½ head Bibb lettuce, leaves separated

TOOLS & EQUIPMENT

Measuring spoons

Knife

Cutting board

Medium skillet

1. **Heat the medium skillet over medium-high heat.**

2. **Cook the ground beef and spices.** Add the oil and ground beef to the skillet and cook for 3 to 4 minutes, or until browned. Break the meat up with a wooden spoon as it cooks. Add the garlic, ginger, scallions, salt, five-spice powder, Sriracha, soy sauce, and honey. Cook for 2 minutes, then take the skillet off the heat.

3. **Assemble the wraps.** Wash and dry the lettuce leaves. Fill the leaves with the ground beef mixture, taco style, and enjoy.

TAKE THE EASY WAY OUT: Cook the beef with a store-bought stir-fry sauce, and you can do away with the five-spice powder, Sriracha, soy sauce, and honey.

HONEY MUSTARD–GLAZED SALMON

In the wilderness of the far north, grizzly bears stalk the rivers and streams for fresh salmon. You, however, can just go to the grocery store. It might not be as picturesque as the northern wilderness, but it is a lot better than getting into an argument with a hungry bear. Though, if you showed the bear how to marinate the salmon in honey mustard, you'd probably have a friend for life. Serve the fish with rice and vegetables, or flake it apart and add it to a salad.

5 Ingredients, Dairy-Free, Gluten-Free, Leftover Friendly, Nut-Free, One Pot

MAKES: *1 serving*

PREP TIME: *5 minutes, plus at least 2 hours to marinate*

COOK TIME: *15 minutes*

1 tablespoon honey

2 tablespoons Dijon mustard

½ teaspoon black pepper

2 teaspoons water

1 (6-ounce) salmon fillet

Canola oil, for oiling the rack

TOOLS & EQUIPMENT

Measuring spoons

Medium zippered plastic bag

Broiler pan with rack

1. **Make the marinade.** Put the honey, mustard, pepper, and water in the medium zippered plastic bag. Seal the bag and shake it until the ingredients are mixed.

2. **Marinate the salmon.** Put the salmon in the bag, gently squeeze the air out of the bag, seal it, and put it in the fridge to marinate for at least 2 hours or up to 24 hours.

3. **Preheat your oven to 375°F.**

4. **Cook the salmon.** Lightly oil the rack of the broiler pan and place the salmon on it. Roast the salmon for 15 to 17 minutes, or until it is no longer translucent in the middle. Serve.

CRISPY HONEY-GARLIC TOFU

Before you skip over this recipe because it has tofu, you should know that this is one of the best recipes in the book. At the very least, it is the most unexpectedly delicious recipe. Do yourself a favor and go vegetarian for the night. You'll be happy you did. Serve the tofu over rice or noodles.

30 Minutes, Dairy-Free, Nut-Free, Vegetarian

MAKES: *1 serving*
PREP TIME: *10 minutes*
COOK TIME: *10 minutes*

½ teaspoon kosher salt

¼ cup cornstarch

1 cup medium-diced firm tofu

2 tablespoons canola oil

1 tablespoon sliced garlic

1 cup thinly sliced vegetables of choice (see Helpful Hint)

1 tablespoon honey

2 tablespoons soy sauce

TOOLS & EQUIPMENT

Measuring spoons

Measuring cups

Knife

Wooden spoon

Cutting board

Large plate

Large nonstick skillet

1. **Prep the tofu.** Mix the salt and cornstarch on the large plate. Roll the tofu dice in the mixture to coat well; let sit for 5 minutes.

2. **Cook the tofu.** Heat the large nonstick skillet over medium-high heat. Add the canola oil and the dusted tofu and cook for 6 to 8 minutes, or until golden brown. Stir the tofu gently every minute or so with the wooden spoon. Add the garlic to the skillet and cook for 30 seconds.

3. **Cook the vegetables.** Add the vegetables to the skillet and cook for 2 minutes.

4. **Finish and serve.** Add the honey and cook for 30 seconds, then add the soy sauce and cook for 1 minute. Serve.

HELPFUL HINT: You can use any fresh vegetables you'd like in this stir-fry, but red bell pepper, bean sprouts, scallions, and snow peas make for a winning combination. Whatever vegetables you choose, slice them all about the same size to total 1 cup. That way, they will cook evenly.

CREAMY BACON AND ROASTED RED PEPPER PASTA

Roasted red peppers add a bit of sweetness and color to just about any dish. You can buy them jarred at any grocery store, and they will last for about a month in the fridge, once opened. Look for a brand of roasted red peppers that doesn't list vinegar in the ingredients, since that drastically changes the flavor of the peppers.

30 Minutes, Nut-Free

MAKES: *1 serving*
PREP TIME: *5 minutes*
COOK TIME: *10 minutes*

3½ ounces linguine
½ cup medium-diced bacon
1 teaspoon sliced garlic
½ cup medium-diced roasted red pepper
¼ cup heavy cream
¼ teaspoon kosher salt
¼ teaspoon black pepper
¼ cup grated Parmesan cheese

TOOLS & EQUIPMENT

Measuring cups/spoons
Knife
Wooden spoon
Cheese grater
Cutting board
Colander
Large pot
Medium skillet

1. **Cook the pasta.** Fill the large pot with water and bring to a boil over high heat. Add the pasta and cook according to the package instructions, about 10 minutes, until tender. Drain in the colander.

2. **Cook the bacon.** Meanwhile, put the bacon in the skillet before heating it, then put the skillet over medium heat. Cook the bacon for 6 to 7 minutes, or until it is crisp. Drain off all the bacon fat except 1 tablespoon.

3. **Cook the aromatics.** Add the garlic and roasted red pepper to the skillet and cook for 2 minutes.

4. **Mix the pasta and cream.** Add the cream to the skillet along with the salt and pepper. With the wooden spoon, stir in the pasta and toss or stir to coat it in the sauce.

5. **Serve.** Put the pasta in a serving bowl, sprinkle with the Parmesan cheese, and enjoy.

KICK IT UP A NOTCH: Toss a handful of fresh spinach into the skillet along with the garlic and roasted red pepper to add some more vegetables.

PAN-FRIED HADDOCK BURGER

Move over, ground beef. See you later, pulled pork. Talk to you never, crispy chicken. There's a new burger in town, and it don't care about nothin'. If it were in a 1980s teen movie, this haddock burger would wear a leather jacket and black shades and ride a motorcycle. It's that cool. And now you can be, too.

30 Minutes, Nut-Free, One Pot

MAKES: *1 serving*
PREP TIME: *5 minutes*
COOK TIME: *10 minutes*

¼ cup all-purpose flour
1 teaspoon Cajun seasoning
¼ teaspoon kosher salt
1 (6-ounce) haddock fillet
1 tablespoon butter
1 teaspoon olive oil
1 burger bun
2 teaspoons mayonnaise
6 dill pickle slices
1 teaspoon hot sauce

TOOLS & EQUIPMENT

Measuring cups/spoons
Knife
Butter knife
Silicone spatula
Cutting board
Large plate
Toaster
Medium nonstick skillet

1. **Dredge the haddock.** On the large plate, combine the flour, Cajun seasoning, and salt. Mix well. Cut the haddock fillet in half crosswise and pat it in the flour to coat well.

2. **Heat the nonstick skillet over medium-high heat.**

3. **Cook the haddock.** Add the butter and olive oil to the skillet. When the butter melts and starts to foam, add the haddock pieces and cook for 2½ to 3 minutes per side, or until the fish browns.

4. **Toast the bun.** While the haddock is cooking, toast the burger bun in the toaster. If your toaster has a bagel setting, use that.

5. **Assemble the burger.** Spread the mayonnaise on both halves of the bun with the butter knife. Put the pickles on the bottom half of the bun and stack the haddock pieces on top. Sprinkle the haddock with the hot sauce, then put on the top bun half and press gently. Serve.

HELPFUL HINT: If you find the flour coating isn't sticking well to the fish in step 1, try coating the fish first in a small bowl with 1 beaten egg, then dredging with the flour.

KICK IT UP A NOTCH: For a blast of flavor, add some pickled jalapeños and a slice of Cheddar cheese to the sandwich.

MUSHROOM RAMEN

Ramen is all the rage, and now you can easily make this vegan version at home. You can also "meatify" it if you want by adding ½ cup diced roasted pork and a sliced soft-boiled egg.

30 Minutes, Dairy-Free, Leftover Friendly, Nut-Free, One Pot, Vegan

MAKES: *1 serving*
PREP TIME: *10 minutes*
COOK TIME: *15 minutes*

3 ounces dried ramen noodles

1 tablespoon canola oil

1 cup sliced fresh mushrooms (see Helpful Hint)

1 teaspoon minced fresh ginger

1 teaspoon minced garlic

2 cups hot water

1 tablespoon soy sauce

¼ teaspoon salt

2 scallions (white and green parts), thinly sliced

¼ cup small-diced firm tofu

TOOLS & EQUIPMENT

Measuring spoons
Measuring cups
Knife
Wooden spoon
Tongs
Large pot
Medium pot

1. **Cook the noodles.** Fill the large pot with water and bring to a boil over high heat. Add the noodles and cook according to the package instructions, about 5 minutes.

2. **Cook the mushrooms.** Heat the medium pot over medium-high heat. Add the canola oil and mushrooms and cook for 1 minute, then add the ginger and garlic and cook for 30 seconds. Pour the hot water into the pot, making sure to scrape the bottom for stuck ginger and garlic bits with the wooden spoon. Add the soy sauce and salt, bring to a boil, turn the heat down to medium-low, and simmer for 5 minutes.

3. **Cook the scallions and tofu.** Add the scallions and tofu to the broth and simmer for 2 minutes.

4. **Serve.** Use the tongs to transfer the noodles to a serving bowl, pour the broth and tofu over them, and serve.

HELPFUL HINT: Use a variety of fresh mushrooms, such as creminis, shiitakes, and king oysters, to add flavor and texture to the broth.

Pork Chop with Mushroom Sauce

Pork chops don't get the respect they deserve. Don't get me wrong; lots of people eat them, but they are often seen as a low-end protein. That opinion is wrong, because a perfectly cooked pork chop can rival the best steak any day. This recipe will prove that to you.

30 Minutes, Gluten-Free, Nut-Free

MAKES: *1 serving*
PREP TIME: *10 minutes*
COOK TIME: *15 minutes*

1 bone-in pork chop, about ½ inch thick

¼ teaspoon kosher salt, or more as needed

⅛ teaspoon black pepper, or more as needed

2 teaspoons canola oil

½ cup sliced fresh mushrooms (any kind)

½ cup sliced onion

1 teaspoon sliced garlic

1 ounce (2 tablespoons) whiskey of choice

½ cup hot water or chicken broth

1 tablespoon butter

TOOLS & EQUIPMENT

Measuring cups/spoons
Knife
Spatula
Tongs
Cutting board
Work plate
Medium skillet with lid

1. **Heat the medium skillet over medium-high heat.**

2. **Sear the pork chop.** Season both sides of the pork chop with the salt and pepper. Heat the canola oil, then add the pork chop and cook for 2 minutes per side. Press gently on the center of the chop with the spatula to ensure even browning.

3. **Cook the mushrooms and onion.** When the pork chop is browned, take it out of the skillet and set it on a plate. Add the mushrooms and onion to the skillet and cook for 2 minutes, stirring every 20 to 30 seconds. Add the garlic, cook for 1 more minute, then pour in the whiskey and cook for 30 seconds. Add the hot water and briefly stir.

4. **Finish the pork chop.** Using the tongs, put the pork chop back into the skillet, put the lid on the pan, turn the heat to medium-low, and simmer for 3 minutes. Transfer the pork back to the plate and turn the heat back up to high. Cook the pan juices for 2 minutes.

5. **Make the sauce.** Take the skillet off the heat, add the butter, and stir until it melts and the sauce thickens. Taste the sauce and adjust the seasoning with salt and pepper as needed, then pour it over the pork chop and enjoy.

Teriyaki Chicken Breast with Roasted Broccoli

When broccoli is roasted, it takes on a unique flavor that is out of this world. And when it is paired with this teriyaki chicken, you've got a winning combination that you'll be happy to eat any day. Serve as is, or with rice or a salad.

5 Ingredients, 30 Minutes, Dairy-Free, Leftover Friendly, Nut-Free, One Pot

MAKES: *1 serving*
PREP TIME: *5 minutes*
COOK TIME: *25 minutes*

2 cups fresh broccoli florets

1 tablespoon olive oil

½ teaspoon salt

⅛ teaspoon black pepper

1 (6-ounce) skinless, boneless chicken breast

2 tablespoons teriyaki sauce, divided

TOOLS & EQUIPMENT

Measuring spoons

Pastry brush

Spatula

Instant-read thermometer

Medium bowl

Sheet pan

Parchment paper

1. **Preheat your oven to 375°F.** Line the sheet pan with parchment paper.

2. **Prep the broccoli.** Put the broccoli in the medium bowl. Add the olive oil, salt, and pepper. Stir the broccoli to coat it with the oil and seasoning, then spread the florets out on the sheet pan.

3. **Bake the chicken and broccoli.** Put the chicken breast on the sheet pan alongside the broccoli and bake for 10 minutes. Take the pan out of the oven and flip the broccoli florets. Brush the chicken with 1 tablespoon of teriyaki sauce. Continue to bake for 7 more minutes. Take the pan out of the oven again, flip the chicken and brush with the remaining 1 tablespoon of teriyaki sauce, then put the pan back in the oven for 7 more minutes.

4. **Check the chicken.** Check the chicken in its thickest part with an instant-read thermometer; the internal temperature should be 165°F. If not, return it to the oven for a few more minutes.

5. **Serve the chicken and broccoli.** Transfer the chicken and broccoli to a plate and serve.

HELPFUL HINT: You can make homemade teriyaki sauce; see page 108.

Smoked Salmon Sushi Bowl

The nori sheet here should be a small smoked nori snack. You can find them at most grocery stores. Alternatively, you can cut a regular nori sheet into four pieces and use one piece, or leave it out together—although the nori really gives this dish that authentic sushi flavor.

Dairy-Free, Nut-Free

MAKES: *1 serving*
PREP TIME: *10 minutes*
COOK TIME: *30 minutes*

½ cup jasmine or sushi rice

¾ cup water

¼ cup shelled fresh edamame

5 thin slices cucumber

¼ cup thinly sliced carrot

2 to 3 ounces smoked salmon

2 teaspoons teriyaki sauce

1 scallion (white and green parts), sliced

1 smoked nori sheet (see headnote)

TOOLS & EQUIPMENT

Measuring spoons

Measuring cups

Knife

Small strainer

Cutting board

Small pot with lid

1. **Cook the rice.** Rinse the rice in the strainer under cold running water until the water runs clear. Put the rice in the small pot along with the water. Bring the water to a boil, turn the heat to low, and cover. Simmer the rice for 20 minutes, then take it off the heat and let it rest for 5 minutes. Different rice brands may require different amounts of water or a slightly shorter cooking time; always read the instructions on the rice package and monitor the pot to be sure the rice isn't sticking to the pot. Transfer the rice to a serving bowl. Rinse out the pot.

2. **Cook the edamame.** Put the edamame in the small pot, cover with water, and bring to a boil over high heat. Boil for 4 minutes, then use the strainer to drain the edamame.

3. **Assemble the bowl.** Fan the cucumber out around the edge of the serving bowl. Put the carrot in the middle of the bowl in a small pile. Add the smoked salmon, spoon the teriyaki sauce over all, and finish with a sprinkle of the scallion slices. Crumble on the nori and enjoy.

KICK IT UP A NOTCH: Add some punch to the bowl with a little wasabi. Also, you can make your own teriyaki sauce by combining ¼ cup soy sauce, 2 tablespoons brown sugar, 1 tablespoon rice vinegar, and 2 tablespoons water in a small pot and boiling it for 2½ minutes. The sauce will keep in the fridge for a few weeks in an airtight container.

STEAK AND MUSHROOM QUESADILLA

A quesadilla is a bit like a taco sandwich. Now doesn't that sound nice? This particular taco sandwich has steak, mushrooms, and jalapeño jack cheese in it. You can throw it together in under 15 minutes, and it is worth every second of that effort.

30 Minutes, Gluten-Free, Nut-Free, One Pot

MAKES: *1 serving*
PREP TIME: *5 minutes*
COOK TIME: *10 minutes*

2 teaspoons canola oil, divided

1 (4-ounce) New York strip steak, thinly sliced

½ cup sliced cremini mushrooms

½ teaspoon kosher salt

⅛ teaspoon black pepper

2 (6-inch) corn tortillas

¼ cup grated jalapeño jack cheese, divided

Salsa of choice, for serving

Sour cream, for serving

TOOLS & EQUIPMENT

Measuring spoons

Measuring cups

Knife

Cheese grater

Silicone spatula

Cutting board

Small bowl

Medium nonstick skillet

1. **Cook the steak and mushrooms.** Put the medium nonstick skillet over medium-high heat, and let it warm for about 3 minutes. Add 1 teaspoon of canola oil, the steak slices, mushrooms, salt, and pepper, and cook for 2 to 3 minutes, or until the steak is browned and the mushrooms are soft.

2. **Re-prep the pan.** Using the silicone spatula, transfer the steak and mushrooms to a small bowl. Wipe out the skillet with a paper towel or damp cloth. Put the skillet back over medium-high heat and add the remaining 1 teaspoon of oil.

3. **Make the quesadilla.** Put 1 tortilla in the pan, and top with half the cheese and all of the steak mixture. Top the steak with the remaining cheese, then add the second tortilla. Cook for 1½ minutes, or until the bottom tortilla browns. Carefully flip the quesadilla over and cook for another 1½ minutes.

4. **Cut and serve.** Take the quesadilla out of the pan, cut into 4 pieces, and serve with salsa and sour cream.

KICK IT UP A NOTCH: Sauté a sliced jalapeño with the steak and mushrooms to add a little spice to the mix.

Penne Arrabbiata

This is one of the simplest and tastiest pasta dishes there is. When you need a quick meal but don't want to sacrifice flavor, turn to this spicy and flavorful combo. You can bulk it up a bit by adding ½ cup fresh baby spinach and slices of cooked chicken, if you want.

5 Ingredients, 30 Minutes,
Leftover Friendly,
Nut-Free, Vegetarian

MAKES: *1 serving*
PREP TIME: *5 minutes*
COOK TIME: *15 minutes*

3½ ounces penne

1 tablespoon olive oil

1 tablespoon minced garlic

½ teaspoon red
    pepper flakes

½ cup tomato puree

2 tablespoons grated
    Parmesan cheese

¼ teaspoon kosher salt

⅛ teaspoon black pepper

TOOLS & EQUIPMENT

Measuring spoons

Measuring cups

Knife

Wooden spoon

Cheese grater

Cutting board

Colander

Large pot

Medium skillet

1. **Cook the pasta.** Fill the large pot with water and bring to a boil. Add the pasta and cook according to the package instructions, about 10 minutes, or until tender. Drain the pasta in the colander and save ¼ cup of the pasta water.

2. **Cook the aromatics.** Heat the medium skillet over medium-high heat. Add the olive oil, garlic, and red pepper flakes. Cook for 1 to 2 minutes.

3. **Cook the tomato puree.** Add the tomato puree and reserved pasta water to the skillet. Turn the heat down to medium-low and simmer for 3 minutes.

4. **Add the pasta and cheese.** Take the skillet off the heat and add the pasta. Stir with the wooden spoon to combine, then add the Parmesan, salt, and pepper, tossing to coat the pasta with the sauce. Serve.

SUPERSIZE IT: This is an easy recipe to double, triple, or even quadruple. It is the perfect meal for when you have a few people coming over and need something quick and delicious to feed them.

MAC AND CHEESE

Throw away that boxed macaroni and cheese and get to cooking. This recipe takes only a few minutes more to make than the processed stuff, and the taste is no comparison. What's more, you can make it as cheesy as you want. The only question you have to ask yourself is, how much cheese is too much cheese?

30 Minutes, Leftover Friendly, Nut-Free, Vegetarian

MAKES: *1 serving*
PREP TIME: *5 minutes*
COOK TIME: *15 minutes*

3 ounces macaroni

1 tablespoon butter

1 tablespoon all-purpose flour

1 cup whole milk

½ cup grated Cheddar cheese

2 tablespoons grated Parmesan cheese

½ teaspoon kosher salt

⅛ teaspoon black pepper

TOOLS & EQUIPMENT

Measuring spoons

Measuring cups

Whisk

Colander

Cheese grater

Large pot

Medium skillet

1. **Cook the pasta.** Fill the large pot with water and bring to a boil over high heat. Add the pasta and cook according to the package instructions, about 10 minutes, or until tender. Drain in the colander.

2. **Make the cheese sauce.** While the pasta is cooking, heat the medium skillet over medium heat. Add the butter and wait until it melts, then whisk in the flour and cook, stirring, for 2 minutes. Add the milk and cook, gently whisking, for 5 minutes. Whisk in the Cheddar and Parmesan cheeses, salt, and pepper; stir gently until the cheese is melted.

3. **Mix the pasta and the sauce.** Add the macaroni to the sauce in the skillet, and toss or stir to coat the noodles. Serve.

HACK IT 5 WAYS

Consider this mac and cheese a blank canvas. Yes, it is bomb on its own, but you can also add other ingredients to make it even better:
(1) You can throw a few tablespoons of cooked, chopped bacon in there.
(2) You can add a few tablespoons of cooked lobster meat.
(3) You can add 1 tablespoon of blue cheese to the cheese mixture.
(4) You can put the mac and cheese in a small oven-safe dish, top it with a mixture of ¼ cup dried fine bread crumbs, 2 tablespoons grated Parmesan cheese, and 1 tablespoon melted garlic butter, then broil it for 2 to 3 minutes on high, or until the bread crumbs brown.
(5) You can sauté some diced jalapeño in the butter and oil before adding the flour to spice things up a little.

Sweet-and-Sour Chicken Balls · **PAGE 131**

CHAPTER 6

MEALS FOR MORE

SWEET POTATO AND PINTO BEAN ENCHILADAS

Enchiladas are superb when you have people coming over for dinner. You can make them earlier in the day, then put them in the oven right before your guests arrive. Serve them with a salad, and you've got a full meal. If you'd like to add some meat to the enchiladas, a tablespoon or two of Mexican-Style Pulled Pork (page 129) is the perfect addition.

Gluten-Free, Leftover Friendly, Nut-Free, Vegetarian

MAKES: *6 servings*
PREP TIME: *20 minutes*
COOK TIME: *1 hour*

1 pound sweet potatoes

2 tablespoons butter

2 tablespoons all-purpose flour

2 cups whole milk

2 cups grated pepper jack cheese, divided

½ teaspoon salt

2 teaspoons lime juice

12 (6-inch) corn tortillas

1 (15.5-ounce) can pinto beans, drained and rinsed

¾ cup salsa of choice

Lime wedges, for serving

1. **Cook the sweet potatoes.** Put the sweet potatoes in the large pot, cover with water, and bring to a boil over high heat. Boil until you can easily stick a fork through them, about 20 minutes. Drain, then let the sweet potatoes sit until they are cool enough to handle. Peel the sweet potatoes and cut them into ½-inch-wide strips.

2. **Heat the butter, flour, and milk.** Melt the butter in the medium pot over medium heat. Whisk in the flour and cook for 2 minutes. Add the milk and cook for 10 minutes, whisking gently the whole time.

3. **Whisk in half the cheese and salt.** Whisk 1 cup of cheese and the salt into the sauce. Take the pot off the heat and whisk in the lime juice. Put the lid on the pot to keep the sauce warm.

4. **Preheat your oven to 375°F.** Pour one-third of the warm sauce into the 9-by-13-inch baking dish.

5. **Assemble the enchiladas.** Wrap the tortillas in a clean kitchen towel and warm them in the microwave for 1 minute. Place 1 piece of sweet potato, 2 tablespoons of beans, and 1 tablespoon of salsa on each tortilla. Roll up the tortillas and place them in the baking dish.

Measuring spoons

Measuring cups

Knife

Whisk

Cheese grater

Cutting board

Colander

Large pot

Medium pot with lid

9-by-13-inch baking dish

6. **Bake.** Cover the enchiladas with the remaining cheese sauce. Sprinkle with the remaining 1 cup of cheese. Bake for 30 minutes, until bubbly. Let rest for 5 minutes before serving. Serve with a lime wedge on the side.

KICK IT UP A NOTCH: For a little extra heat, add a few slices of fresh or pickled jalapeños to the enchiladas as you roll them. Or, serve the enchiladas with your favorite hot sauce.

MEATBALLS WITH ONION GRAVY

These meatballs in an onion gravy are the ultimate comfort food, especially when they are served with Perfect Mashed Potatoes (page 61). Every bite feels like a big hug from home. You can change the recipe a little by simmering the meatballs in tomato sauce instead, then serving them over pasta or in a sub roll with melted mozzarella.

Leftover Friendly, Nut-Free

MAKES: *4 servings*
PREP TIME: *20 minutes*
COOK TIME: *30 minutes*

1 pound lean ground beef

1 tablespoon dried Italian seasoning

1 teaspoon kosher salt, or more as needed

¼ teaspoon black pepper

2 tablespoons butter

2 cups sliced onions

1 tablespoon all-purpose flour

½ cup dry red wine

2 cups beef broth

1. **Preheat your oven to 400°F.** Line the sheet pan with parchment paper.

2. **Make the meatballs.** In the medium bowl, combine the ground beef, Italian seasoning, salt, and pepper. Mix well. Measure the meat into small portions using a tablespoon. Roll the portions into balls. You should have about 24 meatballs. Put the meatballs on the lined sheet pan and roast for 12 minutes.

3. **Make the gravy.** While the meatballs are cooking, heat the large skillet over medium-high heat. Add the butter and onions. Cook until the onions soften, about 3 minutes.

4. **Flavor the onions.** Sprinkle the flour over the onions and stir until you can't see any white flour anymore. Cook, stirring with the wooden spoon, for 1 minute, then add the wine and cook for another minute. Stir in the broth, bring to a boil, then turn the heat down to low and simmer for 5 minutes.

5. **Add the meatballs to the gravy.** Add the meatballs to the onion gravy, put a lid on the skillet and simmer for 10 minutes. Remove the lid and dip a metal spoon in the gravy, then draw a line on the back of the spoon with your finger. If the line stays, the gravy is ready; if the line disappears, keep simmering the gravy, lid off, for another 5 minutes.

TOOLS & EQUIPMENT

Measuring spoons

Measuring cups

Knife

Wooden spoon

Large metal spoon

Cutting board

Medium bowl

Large skillet with lid

Sheet pan

Parchment paper

6. **Taste and season the gravy.** Taste the gravy and add salt if desired. Transfer the meatballs to individual plates and spoon the gravy over top.

SUPERSIZE IT: Because the meatballs themselves have so few ingredients, you can multiply this recipe easily. For example, double or triple the recipe, roast the meatballs, and then freeze them so you always have some when the craving strikes.

POT ROAST WITH GRAVY

Nailing the perfect medium-rare beef roast can be really hard for the beginner cook. That's why a pot roast is a better option. First, you can use a cheaper cut of meat. Second, because of the way the roast is cooked, you don't have to worry about over-cooking it; the end result will be perfectly tender.

Dairy-Free, Gluten-Free, Leftover Friendly, Nut-Free

MAKES: *8 servings*

PREP TIME: *15 minutes*

COOK TIME: *3 hours 10 minutes*

---

4 medium onions, cut in half

4 garlic cloves, peeled

4 medium carrots, cut into 2-inch chunks

12 fresh cremini mushrooms, quartered

5 pounds boneless top chuck beef roast

2 teaspoons kosher salt, or more as needed

1 teaspoon black pepper, or more as needed

2 cups dry red wine

3 rosemary sprigs

2 tablespoons cornstarch

2 tablespoons cold water

TOOLS & EQUIPMENT

Measuring cups/spoons

Knife

Whisk

Cutting board

Small bowl

Large, heavy pot with lid

1. **Preheat your oven to 325°F.**

2. **Cook the beef and vegetables.** Put the onions, garlic, carrots, and mushrooms in the bottom of the large, heavy pot or Dutch oven. Season the beef on both sides with the salt and pepper, then put it in the pot on top of the vegetables. Pour the wine down the side of the pot so as not to wash the seasoning off the beef. Put 1 rosemary sprig on either side of the roast and 1 on top. Put the lid on the pot and then put it in the oven and cook for 3 hours. When cooked, take the meat out of the pot and spoon as much of the fat off the top of the cooking liquid as possible.

3. **Make the gravy.** Put the pot on the stove over medium heat. Meanwhile, in the small bowl, whisk together the cornstarch and water. Stir the cornstarch mixture into the liquid in the pot using the wooden spoon and cook, stirring regularly, until the gravy is thick enough to coat the back of the metal spoon. (See page 118 for testing with a spoon.)

4. **Season the gravy and serve.** Taste the gravy and add a little salt and pepper, if needed. Thinly slice the beef and serve with the gravy.

BEEF AND BEAN CHILI

There is no point in being able to cook if you can't make a big pot of chili. It's a rite of passage for every new kitchen dweller. The great thing about chili is that it's always a crowd-pleaser, and for good reason: It's hearty and gives you a reason to eat cornbread. Serve the chili as is, over rice, or topped with Cheddar cheese and sour cream. You can make this chili a day ahead, then reheat it and serve, or you can portion it into containers and freeze it so that it's always there when you want it.

Dairy-Free, Gluten-Free, Leftover Friendly, Nut-Free, One Pot

MAKES: *8 servings*
PREP TIME: *20 minutes*
COOK TIME: *40 minutes*

1 tablespoon olive oil

1 pound ground beef

1 cup medium-diced onion

1 tablespoon minced garlic

1 cup medium-diced green bell pepper

1 jalapeño, thinly sliced and seeds removed

2 tablespoons chili powder

1 (15.5-ounce) can kidney beans, drained and rinsed

1 (24.6-ounce) can tomato puree

1 cup hot water

1 teaspoon kosher salt, or more as needed

¼ teaspoon black pepper, or more as needed

1. **Brown the beef.** Heat the large pot over medium-high heat. Add the oil and beef and cook for about 5 minutes, or until browned.

2. **Cook the vegetables and aromatics.** Turn the heat down to medium, add the onion, and cook for 3 minutes, or until the onion starts to soften. Add the garlic, bell pepper, and jalapeño and cook for 2 minutes. Then, add the chili powder and cook for 30 seconds.

3. **Add the beans.** Using the wooden spoon, stir in the kidney beans, tomato puree, water, salt, and pepper. Bring to a boil, then turn the heat to low and simmer for 30 minutes.

4. **Adjust the seasoning.** Taste the chili and add a bit more salt and pepper if needed.

Continues ➤

BEEF AND BEAN CHILI   Continued

TOOLS & EQUIPMENT

Measuring spoons

Measuring cups

Knife

Wooden spoon

Cutting board

Large pot

HACK IT 5 WAYS

This chili is great on its own, but that doesn't mean it can't be made even better:

(1) Swap out the beef for ground pork, chicken, or turkey.

(2) Add ¼ cup of strong brewed coffee for a more earthy tone.

(3) Add 1 ounce of dark chocolate for greater depth.

(4) Add a pinch of ground cinnamon, which goes well with beef and tomatoes.

(5) Combine the coffee, chocolate, and cinnamon to make this one of the best pots of chili you'll ever have.

LAMB KEBABS WITH TOMATO-CUCUMBER SALAD

Meat on a stick is the international sign for "Party over here." So, let's get the party started. These skewers are just as good roasted in the oven as they are done on the grill. If you do cook them on the grill, soak the bamboo skewers in water for 1 hour before skewering the meat, and grill them at 400°F for 4 to 5 minutes per side. You can eat these skewers as is, with rice and salad on the side, but they are even better wrapped in warm pita bread with cucumber salad and Tzatziki Dip (page 46).

Dairy-Free, Gluten-Free, Leftover Friendly, Nut-Free

MAKES: *6 servings*
PREP TIME: *15 minutes*
COOK TIME: *20 minutes*

2 tablespoons olive oil, divided

1 pound ground lamb

1 tablespoon minced garlic

1½ teaspoons kosher salt, divided

½ teaspoon black pepper, divided

2 tablespoons chopped fresh mint, divided

¼ teaspoon ground cinnamon

2 large tomatoes

1 English cucumber

1. **Preheat your oven to 400°F.** Rub 1 tablespoon of olive oil on the sheet pan.

2. **Season the lamb.** In the medium bowl, combine the lamb, garlic, 1 teaspoon of salt, ¼ teaspoon of pepper, 1 tablespoon of mint, and the cinnamon. Mix well.

3. **Skewer and cook the lamb.** Shape the meat into a log on your cutting board. Divide the log into thirds, then divide each third in half. Holding 1 piece of meat, shape it around a skewer. The whole skewer should be covered in an even layer, except for the bottom 2 inches. Repeat with the remaining portions of meat and the remaining skewers. Wash and dry the bowl.

4. **Roast the skewers.** Put the skewers on the prepared sheet pan and roast in the oven for 12 minutes. Flip and roast on the other side for another 5 minutes.

Continues ━━◖

TOOLS & EQUIPMENT

Measuring spoons

Knife

Cutting board

Medium bowl

6 (12-inch) bamboo skewers

Sheet pan

5. **Make the salad.** While the skewers are roasting, cut the tomatoes in half. Lay the tomato halves flat on your cutting board and cut the halves into 8 wedges each. Put the wedges in the medium bowl. Cut the cucumber in half lengthwise, then cut the halves into ⅛-inch slices, holding the knife at a 45° angle. Put the cucumber slices in the bowl with the tomatoes. Season the salad with the remaining 1 tablespoon of olive oil, 1 tablespoon of mint, ½ teaspoon of salt, and ¼ teaspoon of pepper.

6. **Serve the skewers.** Place the skewers on individual plates and mound some salad alongside each serving.

HELPFUL HINT: Wet your hands frequently while handling the meat; this will help prevent the meat from sticking.

Slow-Roasted Pork Ribs

If you know how to turn on your oven and forget about something for a few hours, you can make ribs. They are not nearly as complicated as some people make them out to be, and this recipe will prove that. Season the ribs, put them in the oven, sauce the ribs, put them back in the oven, eat the ribs. Sounds pretty easy, doesn't it?

Dairy-Free, Gluten-Free, Leftover Friendly, Nut-Free

MAKES: *4 servings*
PREP TIME: *10 minutes*
COOK TIME: *2½ hours*

2 teaspoons kosher salt

1 teaspoon black pepper

1 teaspoon garlic powder

1 teaspoon onion powder

1 teaspoon paprika

¼ teaspoon cayenne

2 teaspoons brown sugar

2 half-racks (2–3 pounds each) baby back pork ribs

½ cup barbecue sauce of choice

TOOLS & EQUIPMENT

Measuring cups/spoons

Paring knife

Knife

Fork

Pastry brush

Cutting board

Small bowl

Broiler pan with rack

1. **Preheat your oven to 325°F.**

2. **Mix the spices.** In the small bowl, combine the salt, pepper, garlic powder, onion powder, paprika, cayenne, and brown sugar. Mix well.

3. **Remove the membrane.** Put the racks of ribs meat-side down on your cutting board. There will be a white membrane holding the meat on the bones. Remove the membrane by lifting a corner of it with a paring knife, grabbing it with a paper towel, and pulling it straight off. It should mostly come off in one big piece.

4. **Roast the ribs.** Rub the rib racks on both sides with the seasoning blend, especially rubbing it into the meat. Set the ribs on the rack of the broiler pan and roast for 2 to 2½ hours. The ribs are done when you stick a fork in them, twist gently, and the meat comes away from the bone easily.

5. **Sauce and brown the ribs.** Brush the rib racks with the barbecue sauce. Turn the oven up to 425°F and put the ribs back in the oven to roast for 5 minutes more, or until the sauce starts to brown. Cut the racks in half and brush the ribs with a little more sauce before serving.

TAKE THE EASY WAY OUT: If you want to make it even simpler, use a store-bought rub or season the ribs with just salt and pepper.

HERB AND GARLIC-ROASTED CHICKEN DRUMSTICKS

This herb- and garlic-infused chicken is deceptively delicious. Like, it shouldn't taste as good as it does with so few ingredients. But it does. The seasoning works just as well on a whole chicken, chicken breasts, or thighs, too. Once you taste this, you'll wonder why you've ever eaten chicken any other way.

5 Ingredients, Dairy-Free, Gluten-Free, Nut-Free

MAKES: *6 servings*
PREP TIME: *10 minutes*
COOK TIME: *30 minutes*

1 tablespoon chopped fresh thyme

1 tablespoon chopped fresh rosemary

1 tablespoon sliced garlic

½ teaspoon red pepper flakes

3 tablespoons olive oil

1 teaspoon kosher salt

¼ teaspoon black pepper

12 chicken drumsticks

TOOLS & EQUIPMENT

Measuring spoons
Knife
Cutting board
Instant-read thermometer
Medium bowl
Sheet pan
Parchment paper

1. **Preheat your oven to 400°F.** Line the sheet pan with parchment paper.

2. **Mix all the ingredients.** In the medium bowl, combine the thyme, rosemary, garlic, red pepper flakes, olive oil, salt, and pepper. Mix well, then add the drumsticks and toss with your hands to coat them in the herb and garlic mixture.

3. **Roast the chicken.** Spread out the drumsticks on the lined sheet pan, leaving a little space between them. Roast for 30 minutes, or until the internal temperature reaches 165°F. Serve.

TAKE THE EASY WAY OUT: Replace the herbs and garlic with 2 tablespoons dried Italian seasoning.

MUSHROOM AND LENTIL STEW

When you think of stew, you probably think of big chunks of meat and vegetables in gravy. It makes perfect sense that you would think that, because that's what stew is. But not this stew. This one is vegan, and it is just as good as any meat stew you've ever had. Enjoy the stew as is, or spoon it over rice or Perfect Mashed Potatoes (page 61).

Dairy-Free, Gluten-Free, Leftover Friendly, Nut-Free, Vegan

MAKES: *6 servings*
PREP TIME: *15 minutes*
COOK TIME: *30 minutes*

2 tablespoons olive oil
1 cup medium-diced onion
1 cup medium-diced carrot
2 cups medium-diced portobello mushroom caps
1 cup sliced cremini mushrooms
1½ teaspoon kosher salt
¼ teaspoon black pepper
1 tablespoon minced garlic
1 tablespoon chopped fresh rosemary
2 tablespoons cornstarch
6 cups cold water
1 cup lentils, rinsed and drained

TOOLS & EQUIPMENT

Measuring cups/spoons
Knife
Large spoon
Cutting board
Medium bowl
Large pot with lid

1. **Cook the vegetables.** Put the large pot on the stove over medium-high heat. Add the olive oil, onion, carrot, and mushrooms and cook for 5 minutes. Stir every minute or so. Add the salt, pepper, garlic, and rosemary to the pot and cook for 1 minute more.

2. **Cook the lentils.** In the medium bowl, whisk the cornstarch into the water, then pour the mixture into the pot. Add the lentils and bring to a boil.

3. **Simmer the stew.** Turn the heat to low, put the lid on the pot, and simmer for 20 minutes, or until the lentils are tender. Stir the stew every few minutes. Serve.

MEXICAN-STYLE PULLED PORK

Pulled pork is obviously one of the best things in the world. That isn't an opinion. It is a fact. Therefore, you should know how to make it. This recipe changes the focus, though, from the traditional smoky barbecued pork to using Mexican *al pastor* flavors instead. You can serve it with corn on the cob or stuff it into a taco, burrito, or sandwich. Either way, it's winner, winner, pork dinner.

Dairy-Free, Gluten-Free, Leftover Friendly, Nut-Free, One Pot

MAKES: *6 servings*
PREP TIME: *20 minutes*
COOK TIME: *3 hours*

4 pounds bone-in
  pork shoulder
1 tablespoon dried oregano
1 teaspoon ground cumin
¼ teaspoon ground
  coriander
2 teaspoons kosher salt
¼ teaspoon black pepper
1 cup sliced onion
2 garlic cloves
1 jalapeño, sliced
1 cup pineapple juice
2 teaspoons apple cider
  vinegar or lime juice

TOOLS & EQUIPMENT

Measuring cups/spoons
2 forks
Instant-read thermometer
Cutting board
Large oven-safe pot with
  lid (such as Dutch oven)

1. **Preheat your oven to 325°F.**

2. **Cook the pork.** Season the pork on both sides with the oregano, cumin, coriander, salt, and pepper. Put the onion, garlic, jalapeño, and pineapple juice in the large pot. Place the pork on top, cover with the lid, and cook in the oven for 3 hours, or until the pork is very tender. An instant-read thermometer stuck in the center should register 200°F.

3. **Rest and pull the pork.** Transfer the meat to a plate to rest and cool for 10 minutes. Then, use 2 forks to pull the meat apart and away from the bone. Discard the bone and any excess fat.

4. **Finish the pork.** Return the shredded meat back to the pot and stir it into the braising liquid. Add the vinegar, stir well, and serve.

HELPFUL HINT: You can also cook the pork in a casserole dish or roasting pan, covered tightly with aluminum foil.

1980s Tuna Noodle Casserole

There was a time when Saturday mornings meant you'd be watching scientists bust ghosts, mutated turtle brothers fight ninjas, and ducks tell tales. Back in those days, if you had a friend over for dinner, there was a good chance that dinner involved tuna noodle casserole. You may or may not have been alive in the '80s. But you can know the pleasure of a tuna noodle casserole, made here with fusilli instead of egg noodles and homemade cream sauce instead of cream of mushroom soup concentrate.

Leftover Friendly, Nut-Free

MAKES: *6 servings*
PREP TIME: *10 minutes*
COOK TIME: *30 minutes*

1 pound fusilli
2 tablespoons olive oil
1 cup small-diced onion
2 cups frozen peas
    and carrots
2 cups heavy cream
2 (5-ounce) cans
    tuna, drained
1 teaspoon kosher salt
¼ teaspoon black pepper
1 teaspoon dried dill
1 cup grated mozzarella
    cheese, divided
2 cups plain potato
    chips, crushed

TOOLS & EQUIPMENT

Measuring cups/spoons
Wooden spoon
Cheese grater
Colander
Large pot
Large oven-safe skillet
    or baking dish

1. **Preheat your oven to 400°F.**

2. **Cook the pasta.** Fill the large pot with water and bring to a boil. Add the fusilli and cook according to package instructions, about 8 minutes, or until tender.

3. **Cook the vegetables.** Heat the large oven-safe skillet over medium-high heat. Add the olive oil and onion and cook for 3 minutes or until the onion is translucent. Add the peas and carrots and cook for 2 more minutes.

4. **Cook the tuna.** Pour in the cream, then add the tuna, salt, pepper, and dill. Bring to a boil, cook for 1 minute, then turn the heat off. Add the fusilli and ½ cup of mozzarella.

5. **Bake the casserole.** Spread the mixture evenly in the skillet (or transfer to a baking dish), then add the remaining ½ cup of mozzarella and top with the crushed potato chips. Bake for 15 minutes or until bubbly.

6. **Serve.** Take the skillet out of the oven, let the casserole rest for 5 minutes, and serve.

KICK IT UP A NOTCH: Use flavored chips instead of plain to add a boost of flavor. Sriracha potato chips are especially delicious.

SWEET-AND-SOUR CHICKEN BALLS

Have you ever sat in a Chinese restaurant, eating the sweet-and-sour chicken balls, and thought to yourself, "Man, I'd really like to be able to eat these every day"? Well, now you can. This recipe gives you the restaurant flavor of those chicken balls without the breading and deep-frying, which pretty much makes them a health food.

Dairy-Free, Gluten-Free, Nut-Free

MAKES: *4 servings*
PREP TIME: *15 minutes*
COOK TIME: *25 minutes*

1 pound ground chicken

1 teaspoon minced garlic

1 teaspoon minced
    fresh ginger

1 teaspoon kosher salt

¼ teaspoon black pepper

¼ cup seedless
    raspberry jam

½ cup white vinegar

½ cup sugar

½ cup cold water

1 tablespoon cornstarch

2 teaspoons canola oil

TOOLS & EQUIPMENT

Measuring cups/spoons

Whisk

Medium bowl

Sheet pan

Large nonstick skillet

Parchment paper

1. **Preheat your oven to 400°F.** Line the sheet pan with parchment paper.

2. **Make the chicken balls.** In the medium bowl, combine the chicken, garlic, ginger, salt, and pepper. Mix well. Use a tablespoon to measure out small portions of the chicken mixture and then roll into balls. You should have about 24 balls.

3. **Cook the meatballs.** Put the chicken balls on the lined sheet pan and bake for 12 minutes. Remove the balls from the oven and set aside. Meanwhile, wash and dry the bowl.

4. **Make the sauce.** In that same bowl, whisk together the jam, vinegar, sugar, water, and cornstarch.

5. **Brown the balls.** Heat the large nonstick skillet over medium-high heat. Pour in the canola oil, then add the chicken balls and brown on all sides, stirring occasionally with the wooden spoon, for about 3 minutes.

6. **Combine the balls and sauce.** Whisk the sauce ingredients again to make sure the cornstarch hasn't settled on the bottom of the bowl, then pour it into the skillet. Turn the heat down to medium-low and simmer the balls in the sauce for 10 minutes, stirring every minute or so.

7. **Serve.** Spoon portions of the chicken balls and some of the sauce onto serving plates.

CHICKPEA AND SWEET POTATO CURRY

The sweetness of sweet potatoes offers the perfect counterbalance to the heat and spiciness of curry powder. Throw in some chickpeas for protein and some green bell pepper for a pop of color, and you have a delicious vegan dish. Serve over rice or with naan to make it a full meal.

Dairy-Free, Gluten-Free, Leftover Friendly, Nut-Free, One Pot, Vegan

MAKES: *6 servings*
PREP TIME: *15 minutes*
COOK TIME: *25 minutes*

2 tablespoons olive oil
1 cup small-diced onion
2 teaspoons minced
    fresh ginger
2 teaspoons minced garlic
1 tablespoon curry powder
4 cups diced sweet potatoes
3 cups water
1 teaspoon kosher salt,
    or more as needed
¼ teaspoon black pepper,
    or more as needed
1 (15.5-ounce) can chickpeas,
    drained and rinsed
1 cup medium-diced
    green bell pepper
2 teaspoons fresh
    lemon juice

TOOLS & EQUIPMENT

Measuring cups/spoons
Knife
Cutting board
Large pot with lid

1. **Cook the onion.** Heat the large pot over medium-high heat. Add the oil and onion and cook for 3 minutes, or until the onion is translucent.

2. **Cook the spices.** Add the ginger and garlic and cook for 1 minute. Then, add the curry powder and cook for 30 seconds more.

3. **Cook the sweet potatoes.** Add the sweet potatoes, water, salt, and pepper, then bring to a boil, put on the lid, and cook for 5 minutes.

4. **Add the chickpeas and green pepper.** Stir in the chickpeas and green pepper and cook for 5 to 10 minutes, or until the sweet potatoes are tender.

5. **Finish the curry.** Add the lemon juice, then taste the curry and add a little more salt and pepper if needed. Serve in individual bowls.

KICK IT UP A NOTCH: Add 2 cups sliced green cabbage and 2 cups diced white potatoes to bulk it up a little bit.

CHICKEN AND RICE PILAF

When you first look over this recipe, it may seem strange to you. Like, why are there prunes in it? Well, the prunes are there to add a pop of sweetness and a little balance for the savory flavors. This dish is going to take you a tad out of your comfort zone, but that isn't a bad thing, is it? You're cooking, after all, and that's out of your old comfort zone. Why not try something completely new while you're at it?

Dairy-Free, Gluten-Free, Leftover Friendly, Nut-Free

MAKES: *6 servings*
PREP TIME: *10 minutes*
COOK TIME: *30 minutes*

1½ cups basmati rice

8 skinless, boneless chicken thighs (about 2 pounds)

2 teaspoons kosher salt, divided

½ teaspoon black pepper, divided

2 tablespoons olive oil, divided

1 cup small-diced onion

1 teaspoon minced garlic

1 tablespoon garam masala

1 cup frozen peas and carrots

½ cup medium-diced prunes

3 cups water or chicken broth

1 lemon, sliced

1. **Rinse the rice.** Put the rice in the medium bowl, cover with cold water, and stir for 30 seconds. Use the strainer to rinse the rice. Repeat this process until the water is clear; set the rice aside.

2. **Heat the large, heavy-bottomed pot over medium-high heat.**

3. **Cook the chicken.** Season the chicken thighs on both sides with 1 teaspoon of salt and ¼ teaspoon of pepper. Put 1 tablespoon of olive oil in the pot, then add half the chicken. Sear on both sides until browned, about 2 minutes per side, then use the tongs to transfer the chicken to the large bowl. Add the remaining chicken to the pot and brown both sides. Add the second batch of chicken to the large bowl.

4. **Cook the aromatics and spices.** Turn the heat down to medium and add the remaining 1 tablespoon of oil and the onion to the pot. Cook for 3 minutes, or until the onion softens. Add the garlic and garam masala and cook, stirring, for 30 seconds.

Continues ➡

CHICKEN AND RICE PILAF Continued

TOOLS & EQUIPMENT

Measuring spoons

Measuring cups

Knife

Wooden spoon

Tongs

Fine-mesh strainer

Medium bowl

Large bowl

Large, heavy-bottomed
pot with lid (such
as Dutch oven)

5. **Simmer the chicken.** Return the chicken to the pot, then add the peas and carrots, prunes, rice, and water. Bring the liquid to a boil, making sure to scrape the bottom so that nothing sticks. Put on the lid, turn the heat down to low, and simmer for 17 minutes, or until the rice is cooked. Take the pot off the heat and let it sit for 10 minutes before serving. Serve on plates with a slice of lemon on the side.

Spiced Lentil-Stuffed Peppers

Stuffed peppers are a cool thing to serve because everyone gets a little edible pepper bowl of goodness. This version is vegetarian, but you'd never know it. In fact, if you don't tell your guests, they probably won't realize there's no meat. If desired, substitute Italian seasoning, Cajun seasoning, or garam masala for the chili powder. The recipe uses cooked rice, so if you don't have any on hand, you'll need to make that first.

Gluten-Free, Leftover Friendly, Nut-Free, Vegetarian

MAKES: *6 servings*
PREP TIME: *20 minutes*
COOK TIME: *50 minutes*

2 tablespoons olive oil, plus more for greasing

½ cup minced onion

1 teaspoon minced garlic

1 (19-ounce) can lentils, drained and rinsed

1 cup cooked basmati rice

½ cup tomato puree

½ cup hot water

½ teaspoon chili powder

1 teaspoon kosher salt

¼ teaspoon black pepper

1 cup large-diced mozzarella, divided

3 bell peppers (any color)

TOOLS & EQUIPMENT

Measuring cups/spoons
Knife
Cutting board
Medium skillet
9-by-13-inch baking dish

1. **Preheat your oven to 375°F.** Lightly coat the baking dish with a little oil.

2. **Sauté the aromatics.** Heat the medium skillet over medium-high heat. Add the olive oil, onion, and garlic and cook for 2 minutes, until the onion is softened.

3. **Make the filling.** Add the lentils, cooked rice, tomato puree, hot water, chili powder, salt, and pepper to the skillet. Cook just until the lentils and rice are hot. Take the skillet off the heat and mix in ½ cup of mozzarella.

4. **Prep and stuff the peppers.** Cut the bell peppers vertically in half through the stem end. Take out the seeds, trim any core, and place the peppers cut side up in the prepared baking dish. Pack each pepper half with the rice-lentil mixture. Top the stuffed peppers with the remaining ½ cup of mozzarella.

5. **Roast the peppers.** Put the baking dish in the oven and bake for 45 minutes, or until the peppers are tender. Serve.

HELPFUL HINT: Use different color peppers to make the dish more visually appealing.

CUBAN-STYLE PORK CHOPS

Throw on some salsa music, mix up a batch of mojitos, cook some rice and beans, and make these pork chops for a great Cuban-themed evening. Or, just make them because it's Tuesday and you like them.

Dairy-Free, Gluten-Free, Leftover Friendly, Nut-Free, One Pot

MAKES: *6 servings*
PREP TIME: *5 minutes, plus overnight to marinate*
COOK TIME: *10 minutes*

½ cup sliced onion

1 tablespoon sliced garlic

½ cup fresh orange juice

2 tablespoons apple cider vinegar

2 tablespoons brown sugar

1 tablespoon chopped fresh thyme

2 teaspoons kosher salt, divided

½ teaspoon black pepper, divided

6 bone-in pork chops, about ½ inch thick

TOOLS & EQUIPMENT

Measuring spoons

Measuring cups

Knife

Cutting board

Large zippered plastic bag

Broiler pan

1. **Marinate the chops.** In a large zippered plastic bag, combine the onion, garlic, orange juice, apple cider vinegar, brown sugar, thyme, 1 teaspoon of salt, and ¼ teaspoon of pepper. Seal the bag and shake to mix. Add the pork chops and gently toss back and forth to coat them with the marinade. Push all the excess air from the bag, seal it, and put it in the fridge to marinate overnight.

2. **Prepare the pork chops.** Turn your oven broiler to high heat. Take the pork chops out of the marinade, pat them dry with a paper towel, and season on both sides with the remaining 1 teaspoon of salt and ¼ teaspoon of pepper.

3. **Cook the pork chops.** Put the chops on the broiler pan. Broil for 4 to 5 minutes, then flip them over and broil for another 4 to 5 minutes, until browned. Serve.

Peanut-Ginger Halibut Skewers

You've seen meat on a stick. Well, buckle your seatbelt, buddy, because this is fish-on-a-stick time, with peanut butter. Yes, you read that right, but don't let it deter you, because you don't want to miss out on this one. The recipe works just as well with scallops and shrimp as it does with the halibut, and you can cook it in the oven or on the grill.

30 Minutes, Dairy-Free

MAKES: *6 servings*
PREP TIME: *10 minutes*
COOK TIME: *10 minutes*

Canola oil, for greasing the rack

¼ cup creamy peanut butter

1 teaspoon minced fresh ginger

1 teaspoon minced garlic

1 tablespoon soy sauce

1 tablespoon brown sugar

¼ teaspoon Thai or Vietnamese fish sauce

¼ cup hot water

1 teaspoon Sriracha

1 pound halibut fillet

1 lime

TOOLS & EQUIPMENT

Measuring cups/spoons

Knife

Whisk

Cutting board

6 (10-inch) skewers

Medium bowl

Broiler pan with rack

1. **Turn your oven broiler to high heat.** Lightly oil the rack of the broiler pan.

2. **Make the sauce.** In the medium bowl, combine the peanut butter, ginger, garlic, soy sauce, brown sugar, fish sauce, hot water, and Sriracha. Whisk until it doesn't look gross anymore. Seriously, it's going to look disgusting for a minute, but it will come together and look delicious.

3. **Season the halibut.** Cut the halibut into ½-inch-wide strips, then put the strips in the peanut sauce and turn them to coat well.

4. **Skewer and cook the halibut.** Thread the halibut strips on the skewers, and place the skewers on the broiler rack. Broil the halibut for 5 minutes, then flip the skewers and cook for 5 more minutes.

5. **Serve.** Place the skewers on serving plates. Cut the lime in half and squeeze the juice over the skewers. Serve.

HELPFUL HINT: If using bamboo skewers, soak them in water for 1 hour ahead so they don't smoke up your house.

Bacon-Wrapped Pork Tenderloin with Cola Barbecue Sauce

What kind of cookbook would this be if there weren't at least one recipe for something wrapped in bacon? No kind of cookbook, that's what kind. Keep in mind that this recipe is only as good as the bacon you buy, so don't cheap out. Get the good stuff. Same with the cola.

Dairy-Free, Gluten-Free, Leftover Friendly, Nut-Free

MAKES: *6 servings*
PREP TIME: *20 minutes*
COOK TIME: *35 minutes*

1 pound sliced bacon

½ teaspoon kosher salt, divided

½ teaspoon black pepper, divided

2 pork tenderloins (3–4 pounds total)

¼ cup cola soda

½ cup ketchup

1 tablespoon apple cider vinegar

⅛ teaspoon cayenne pepper

1 teaspoon canola oil

1. **Preheat your oven to 400°F.**

2. **Wrap the tenderloins in bacon.** Place a 12-inch piece of plastic wrap across your cutting board. Arrange half the bacon strips in a neat row, slightly overlapping. Season the bacon with ¼ teaspoon of salt and ¼ teaspoon of pepper. Lay one of the tenderloins on one end of the bacon strips, and roll it forward, using the plastic wrap to keep the bacon in place. Roll until the other end of the bacon strips is on the bottom of the tenderloin, sealing the wrap. Repeat the process with the remaining bacon and second tenderloin.

3. **Make the barbecue sauce.** In the medium bowl, whisk together the cola, ketchup, vinegar, remaining ¼ teaspoon of salt, remaining ¼ teaspoon of pepper, and cayenne.

4. **Brown the bacon.** Heat the large nonstick skillet over medium-high heat. Add the canola oil and then the tenderloins, being sure the side with the bacon ends is facing down. Cook for 2 to 3 minutes, or until the bacon is browned. This should also help secure the bacon strips in place. Flip the tenderloins, and brown on the other side for another 2 minutes.

TOOLS & EQUIPMENT

Measuring spoons

Measuring cups

Whisk

Pastry brush

Cutting board

Medium bowl

Large nonstick skillet

Broiler pan with rack

Plastic wrap

5. **Sauce and roast the tenderloins.** Place the tenderloins on the rack set above the broiler pan, being sure the ends of the bacon are facing down. Brush the tenderloins with some of the barbecue sauce. Roast in the oven for 15 minutes, then brush the tenderloins with more sauce and roast for 15 more minutes, or until the internal temperature of the pork reaches 145°F.

6. **Rest the pork, then slice.** Brush the tenderloins with any remaining sauce and let them rest for 5 minutes. Slice the pork into ¼-inch-thick slices and serve.

TAKE THE EASY WAY OUT: Use a store-bought sauce rather than making your own.

TOFU PASTA BAKE

Just because you are a meat eater, that doesn't mean you can't also sometimes be a tofu eater. As much as you probably don't want to, you should give this recipe a shot. You won't miss the meat, and you'll be surprised at how good it is.

Leftover Friendly,
Nut-Free, Vegetarian

MAKES: *6 servings*
PREP TIME: *10 minutes*
COOK TIME: *40 minutes*

1 pound penne pasta
2 tablespoons olive oil
1 cup small-diced onion
2 cups fresh or frozen
   broccoli florets
1 cup sliced mushrooms
1 tablespoon sliced garlic
1 teaspoon kosher salt
2 tablespoons Italian
   seasoning
1 (24.5-ounce) can
   tomato puree
1 cup hot water
2 cups medium-diced
   firm tofu
1 cup grated mozzarella

TOOLS & EQUIPMENT

Measuring cups/spoons
Wooden spoon
Cheese grater
Cutting board
Colander
Large pot
Large oven-safe skillet

1. **Preheat your oven to 400°F.**

2. **Cook the pasta.** Fill the large pot with water and bring to a boil. Add the pasta and cook for 2 minutes less than the package instructions say, then drain in the colander.

3. **Cook the aromatics and vegetables.** Heat the large skillet over medium-high heat. Add the olive oil, onion, and broccoli and cook for 3 minutes. Add the mushrooms, garlic, and salt and cook for another 2 minutes. Add the Italian seasoning, tomato puree, and hot water. Then, turn the heat down to medium-low and simmer for 5 minutes.

4. **Mix and bake.** Add the pasta and tofu to the sauce, sprinkle it with the mozzarella, and transfer the skillet to the oven. Bake for 20 minutes, or until the cheese is melted and brown on top.

5. **Serve the pasta.** Let the pasta dish rest for 5 minutes before digging in.

HELPFUL HINT: Use the hot water to rinse out the container the tomato puree came in, then pour it into the sauce.

PEA AND PROSCIUTTO PASTA

It's 6 p.m. There's a knock on your door. Five of your friends unexpectedly drop by for dinner. What do you do? You run into the kitchen, throw a pot of water on the stove, cut up some onion, garlic, and prosciutto, and have a kick-ass meal ready in minutes.

30 Minutes, Nut-Free

MAKES: *6 servings*
PREP TIME: *10 minutes*
COOK TIME: *10 minutes*

1 pound linguine
8 slices prosciutto
2 tablespoons olive oil
1 cup small-diced onion
1 tablespoon sliced garlic
1 cup frozen peas
1 cup heavy cream
¼ teaspoon kosher salt
¼ teaspoon black pepper
1 cup grated Parmesan cheese, divided

TOOLS & EQUIPMENT

Measuring spoons
Measuring cups
Knife
Wooden spoon
Cheese grater
Cutting board
Colander
Large pot
Large skillet

1. **Make the pasta.** Fill the large pot with water and bring to a boil over high heat. Add the pasta and cook according to package instructions. Drain the pasta in a colander.

2. **Prep the prosciutto.** Meanwhile, pull the slices of prosciutto apart and cut them in half lengthwise. Then, cut those strips into ¼-inch pieces.

3. **Cook the prosciutto and peas.** Heat the large skillet over medium-high heat. Add the olive oil and onion and cook for 2 minutes. Add the prosciutto and cook for 2 more minutes. Stir in the garlic and peas. Cook for 1 minute, then add the cream, salt, and pepper. Bring everything to a boil, then turn the heat down to medium-low and simmer for 3 minutes.

4. **Mix the pasta and sauce.** Add the pasta and ½ cup of Parmesan to the sauce; toss or stir to coat the pasta. Top with the remaining ½ cup of Parmesan and serve.

SOUTHERN SEAFOOD BOIL

You don't have to live in the South to enjoy a good Southern seafood boil every now and again. Cook this on a hot summer day and eat it outside in the sunshine, along with an ice-cold beer. That's an A+ day right there.

Gluten-Free, Nut-Free, One Pot

MAKES: *6 servings*
PREP TIME: *10 minutes*
COOK TIME: *20 minutes*

2 tablespoons butter

1 cup sliced onion

1 teaspoon sliced garlic

3 cups water

3 ears of corn, husked, silks removed, and cut in half

8 ounces baby yellow potatoes, cut in half

2 teaspoons Old Bay seasoning

¼ teaspoon red pepper flakes

3 pounds mixed fresh seafood (shrimp, scallops, mussels)

TOOLS & EQUIPMENT

Measuring spoons

Measuring cups

Knife

Wooden spoon

Cutting board

Large pot with lid

1. **Cook the onion and garlic.** Heat the large pot over medium heat and add the butter. When the butter melts and starts to foam, add the onion and cook for 3 minutes. Then, add the garlic and cook for 1 minute more.

2. **Boil the corn and potatoes.** Pour the water into the pot and add the corn, potatoes, Old Bay seasoning, and red pepper flakes. Put the lid on the pot and cook for 10 minutes.

3. **Cook the seafood.** Add the seafood to the pot, put the lid back on, and cook until the seafood is done, 4 to 5 minutes. Serve in individual bowls.

HELPFUL HINT: Serve this seafood boil with some garlic-parsley butter as a dip. In a small bowl, combine 4 tablespoons melted butter, 1 crushed garlic clove, and 2 tablespoons chopped parsley.

KICK IT UP A NOTCH: You could make this already tasty combination even better by adding 6 blue-claw crabs, cleaned and ready. They take a bit longer to cook, so you'll want to add them to the pot along with the potatoes and corn.

Strawberry Napoleon · **PAGE 152**

BANANAS FOSTER

The elegant Brennan's restaurant, in New Orleans, originated this dessert. Bananas foster is an older, cooler, more sophisticated sibling of the banana split. If they were people, the banana split would be sucking on a lollipop, wearing overalls and a beanie with a propeller on it. Bananas foster would be wearing a sports jacket and smoking a cigar while regaling you with stories of the time they discovered buried treasure on a 60-day voyage on their baller yacht. Who do you want to be?

30 Minutes, Gluten-Free, Nut-Free, One Pot, Vegetarian

MAKES: *2 servings*
PREP TIME: *5 minutes*
COOK TIME: *5 minutes*

---

2 tablespoons butter

2 tablespoons brown sugar

2 medium bananas, peeled and halved lengthwise

1 ounce (2 tablespoons) dark rum

¼ teaspoon ground cinnamon

2 scoops vanilla ice cream

TOOLS & EQUIPMENT

Measuring spoons

Knife

Silicone spatula

Ice cream scoop

Cutting board

Medium nonstick skillet

Barbecue lighter

1. **Melt the butter and brown sugar.** Heat the medium nonstick skillet over medium heat. Add the butter and brown sugar and wait for the brown sugar to melt.

2. **Cook the bananas.** Add the bananas and cook for 1 minute. Flip with the spatula and cook for another minute.

3. **Light the bananas on fire.** Pour the rum over the bananas and ignite the alcohol with the barbecue lighter. Stand back, unless you're not a fan of your eyebrows. When the flames die back, sprinkle on the cinnamon and shut off the heat.

4. **Serve the bananas with ice cream.** Put the bananas in serving bowls, top each serving with a scoop of ice cream, and then drizzle on the sauce from the skillet.

HELPFUL HINT: If you are using a gas burner, take the skillet off the heat, add the rum, then put it back on the heat. The rum will probably light on its own.

FRUIT CRUMBLE

A crumble is always a crowd-pleaser. It's baked fruit with a sweet and slightly crunchy topping. How could you not love that? Crumbles can be baked a day ahead and then reheated, which makes them a top-notch choice for dinner parties. They also freeze well once baked. This is best served with ice cream or whipped cream.

Leftover Friendly,
Nut-Free, Vegetarian

MAKES: *6 servings*
PREP TIME: *15 minutes*
COOK TIME: *35 minutes*

---

8 tablespoons (1 stick) butter, room temperature

1 cup old-fashioned rolled oats

1 cup all-purpose flour

½ cup brown sugar

5 cups frozen chopped or sliced fruit of choice

3 tablespoons cornstarch

¼ cup granulated sugar

TOOLS & EQUIPMENT

Measuring spoons

Measuring cups

Wooden spoon

2 medium bowls

9-by-13-inch baking dish

1. **Preheat your oven to 375°F.** Lightly coat the 9-by-13-inch baking dish with a bit of the butter.

2. **Make the crumble topping.** In one medium bowl, combine the oats, flour, brown sugar, and butter. Use your hands to push the flour and oats into the butter, and keep working the mixture until the butter is crumbled and coated with the dry ingredients.

3. **Make the fruit filling.** In the other medium bowl, combine the fruit, cornstarch, and granulated sugar. Mix well, then pour the mixture into the baking dish.

4. **Bake the crumble.** Top the fruit with the crumble mixture, transfer the baking dish to the oven, and bake for 35 minutes, until slightly bubbly. Let the crumble rest for 5 minutes, then serve.

HELPFUL HINT: You can use any frozen fruit or fruit mixture in the crumble. You can also use fresh apples, peaches, or pears; just peel, core, and slice the fruit so the pieces are all the same size.

LIME CHEESECAKE

Who said making a cheesecake needs to be difficult? If you can use a hand mixer and boil water, you can make this. Seriously, you can, and you should. This cheesecake is fine served as is, but you could also top it with whipped cream.

Leftover Friendly,
Nut-Free, Vegetarian

MAKES: *6 servings*

PREP TIME: *40 minutes,*
plus 2 hours to chill

COOK TIME: *10 minutes*

---

4 tablespoons (½ stick)
  butter, melted

1 cup graham cracker
  crumbs

1 (3-ounce) package
  lime-flavored gelatin
  dessert mix

1 cup boiling water

1 ice cube

1 (8-ounce) package cream
  cheese, softened

½ cup heavy cream

1 teaspoon vanilla extract

¾ cup confectioners' sugar

TOOLS & EQUIPMENT

Measuring cups/spoons

Knife

Wooden spoon

2 medium bowls

Hand mixer

10-inch pie plate

Plastic wrap

1. **Preheat your oven to 350°F.**

2. **Make the crust.** Combine the butter and graham cracker crumbs in one medium bowl, then press the mixture into the bottom of the 10-inch pie plate. Bake for 10 minutes. Let the crust cool to room temperature, about 30 minutes.

3. **Make the gelatin flavoring.** Combine the gelatin mix with the boiling water, stir well, and let it cool for about 10 minutes. Then, add the ice cube to help firm up the gelatin.

4. **Make the cream cheese filling.** Put the cream cheese in the other medium bowl and beat it on high with the hand mixer until it is smooth, about 3 minutes. Then, turn the mixer to low speed and add the cream. Mix until the cream is fully incorporated into the cream cheese. Add the vanilla, then beat in the confectioners' sugar ¼ cup at a time. When all the sugar is incorporated, stir in the gelatin.

5. **Assemble the pie.** Gently pour the filling into the pie plate , cover with plastic wrap, and put in the fridge to set for at least 2 hours (overnight is better).

6. **Serve the cheesecake.** Cut the cake into wedges and serve.

HELPFUL HINT: Use different flavors of gelatin mix to make this dessert your own.

EASY COCONUT CREAM PIE

You're a beginner cook. You have invited some skeptical friends over for dinner. They are impressed with the first course. They are pleasantly surprised by the main course, too. But dessert, this coconut cream pie, steals the show. They'll never believe you made it yourself.

Leftover Friendly, Vegetarian

MAKES: *6 servings*

PREP TIME: *45 minutes, plus 30 minutes to chill*

COOK TIME: *10 minutes*

¼ cup (½ stick) butter, melted

1 cup graham cracker crumbs

1 cup sweetened coconut flakes

2 cups milk

1 (3.9-ounce) package instant vanilla pudding mix

1 cup heavy cream

1 tablespoon sugar

1. **Preheat your oven to 350°F.** Line the sheet pan with parchment paper.

2. **Make the crust.** In one medium bowl, combine the butter and graham cracker crumbs. Press the mixture into the bottom of the 10-inch pie plate. Bake for 10 minutes, then let the crust cool to room temperature, about 30 minutes. Keep the oven on.

3. **Toast the coconut.** While the crust is cooling, spread the coconut on the sheet pan and bake for 10 minutes, stirring halfway through. Let the coconut cool to room temperature, about 15 minutes.

4. **Make the pudding.** Pour the milk into another medium mixing bowl, then beat in the pudding with the hand mixer set at low speed. When all the powder is incorporated, turn the speed up to high and beat for 2 minutes.

5. **Make the pie.** Mix half the cooled coconut flakes into the pudding mixture, then pour that into the pie crust.

6. **Whip the cream.** Pour the cream into the third medium bowl. Add the sugar and beat the cream with the hand mixer on high speed for 3 to 4 minutes, or until the cream has stiffened and stands up on its own when you pull the beaters away from it.

Continues ➖🍴

EASY COCONUT CREAM PIE   Continued

TOOLS & EQUIPMENT

Measuring spoons

Measuring cups

Wooden spoon

Large metal spoon

3 medium bowls

Hand mixer

10-inch pie plate

Sheet pan

Parchment paper

7. **Finish and chill the pie.** Spread the cream on top of the filling in an even layer. Sprinkle the remaining coconut over the cream, and put the pie in the fridge to set for 30 minutes before serving.

HELPFUL HINT: Bake the coconut flakes and the crust at the same time to cut down on prep time.

HACK IT 5 WAYS

The great thing about using instant pudding mix as the base of this pie is that it opens up a world of possibilities:

(1) Replace the coconut flakes with sliced bananas.

(2) Switch the vanilla pudding for chocolate pudding mix.

(3) Use both chocolate pudding mix and bananas instead of vanilla pudding mix and coconut flakes.

(4) Use a double batch of butterscotch pudding mix and no coconut or bananas.

(5) Melt 1 cup of smooth peanut butter in the microwave for 2 minutes, pour it onto the crust, and put it in the fridge to chill; top with chocolate pudding and whipped cream.

Cardamom-Spiced Yogurt with Pistachios and Honey

At first glance, this recipe may seem too simple to be in a cookbook. Maybe it is. But have you thought of mixing yogurt with cardamom, honey, and pistachios? No. Well, then you'll be glad this recipe's in here when you taste it. Oh, and cardamom is a common baking spice that you can find in the spice aisle of most grocery stores.

5 Ingredients, 30 Minutes, Gluten-Free, Leftover Friendly, One Pot, Vegetarian

MAKES: *4 servings*

PREP TIME: *5 minutes*

2 cups plain Greek yogurt

½ teaspoon ground cardamom

4 tablespoons honey, divided

4 tablespoons minced pistachios, divided

TOOLS & EQUIPMENT

Measuring spoons

Measuring cups

Large spoon

Whisk

Medium bowl

1. **Make the cardamom yogurt.** Put the yogurt in the medium bowl and whisk in the cardamom. Divide the yogurt among 4 small serving dishes.

2. **Top the yogurt.** Drizzle 1 tablespoon of honey over the yogurt in each bowl. Then, sprinkle with 1 tablespoon of pistachios.

3. **Serve.** Enjoy immediately, or cover with plastic wrap and let rest in the fridge for up to 2 hours.

STRAWBERRY NAPOLEON

A strawberry napoleon may seem like a complex thing to make. But, really, all you're doing is baking some premade pastry, slicing some berries, whipping some cream, and stacking it all together. Think of this as a fancy strawberry shortcake. Top it with a dusting of powdered sugar before serving, if desired.

5 Ingredients, Nut-Free, Vegetarian

MAKES: *4 servings*
PREP TIME: *10 minutes, plus 20 minutes to cool*
COOK TIME: *20 minutes*

1 sheet frozen puff pastry, defrosted

1 cup heavy cream

2 tablespoons sugar

1 teaspoon vanilla extract

1½ cups sliced fresh strawberries

1. **Preheat your oven to 400°F.** Line one sheet pan with parchment paper.

2. **Bake the puff pastry.** Unfold and place the sheet of puff pastry on the lined sheet pan. Poke the dough 10 to 12 times with the fork. Cover the pastry with another piece of parchment paper and top with the second sheet pan. Bake for 15 minutes, then remove the top sheet pan and parchment paper and bake the pastry for another 5 to 7 minutes, or until it is lightly browned. Take the pastry out of the oven and put it on the rack to cool to room temperature.

3. **Whip the cream.** In the medium bowl, combine the cream, sugar, and vanilla. Beat with the hand mixer for 2 to 3 minutes, or until the cream is so stiff that you can flip the bowl upside down and the cream doesn't come out.

4. **Cut the pastry.** Cut the edges of the cooled pastry to square them off for presentation. Discard the extra pastry. Cut the remaining pastry into 3 even rectangles, then cut each rectangle into fourths, making 12 small rectangles.

Measuring spoons

Measuring cups

Knife

Fork

Whisk

Cutting board

Hand mixer

Medium bowl

Plate

2 sheet pans

Cooling rack

Parchment paper

5. **Make the napoleon.** Place one of the pastry rectangles on the plate. Top with the whipped cream, strawberries, and a second piece of pastry. Repeat the layers one more time so you have 3 pastry rectangles, ending with strawberries on top. Repeat the layering process with the remaining rectangles and serve right away.

HELPFUL HINT: If you are having people over for dinner, bake the pastry in the morning, cool it to room temperature, cut it, and wrap it in plastic until you are ready to layer it. You can also have the cream whipped and chilling in the fridge for up to 1 hour before serving. The strawberries can be sliced ahead of time, too. That way, when it's time for dessert, everything is ready to go. You just need to assemble it.

LEMON PANNA COTTA

Panna cotta is sweetened cream set with gelatin. It comes off as an impressive dessert to anyone who has never made it before. Really, though, it's easy to make. You can find gelatin in the baking aisle at the grocery store. Serve these ramekins as is or accompanied by fresh berries.

Gluten-Free, Leftover Friendly, Nut-Free, Vegetarian

MAKES: *6 servings*
PREP TIME: *10 minutes, plus 2 hours to chill*
COOK TIME: *10 minutes*

¼ cup cold water

1 (1-ounce) package unflavored gelatin powder

1 cup whole milk

1 cup heavy cream

Grated zest of 1 lemon

⅓ cup sugar

½ teaspoon vanilla extract

TOOLS & EQUIPMENT

Measuring spoons

Measuring cups

Whisk

Fine-mesh strainer

Grater

Medium bowl

Medium pot

6 ramekins or small glasses (½-cup volume)

Plastic wrap

1. **Dissolve the gelatin.** Put the cold water in the medium bowl and sprinkle the gelatin over it. Stir and let sit for 5 minutes to soften.

2. **Make the cream.** In the medium pot, combine the milk, cream, lemon zest, sugar, and vanilla. Bring to a boil over medium-high heat. As soon as the mixture starts to boil, take the pot off the heat.

3. **Combine the cream and gelatin.** Pour the hot cream mixture through the fine-mesh strainer into the bowl with the gelatin; whisk to combine.

4. **Mold and chill.** Pour the mixture into the 6 ramekins or glasses. Cover with plastic wrap and refrigerate for 2 hours.

5. **Serve the panna cotta.** Serve cold. If you want to get really fancy, dip each ramekin in hot water for 30 to 40 seconds, put a plate on top, and invert it. Give it a little shake, and the panna cotta should come right out onto the plate.

HELPFUL HINT: Use a vegetable peeler to zest the lemon, but make sure not to cut too deeply. Any white on the inside of the lemon zest should be scraped off with a knife before using it, since this pith may turn the panna cotta bitter.

Homemade Chocolate Pudding

Nobody makes pudding from scratch anymore. That is precisely why this recipe is here. If you want to dazzle your mom, dad, friends, or whomever, make them homemade chocolate pudding. The hardest part will be convincing them that you made it from scratch.

5 Ingredients, Gluten-Free, Leftover Friendly, Nut-Free, Vegetarian

MAKES: *6 servings*

PREP TIME: *5 minutes, plus 2 hours to chill*

COOK TIME: *10 minutes*

½ cup whole milk

2 tablespoons cornstarch

1½ cups heavy cream

½ teaspoon vanilla extract

2 cups milk chocolate chips

TOOLS & EQUIPMENT

Measuring spoons

Measuring cups

Metal spoon

Whisk

Silicone spatula

Medium microwave-safe bowl

Medium pot

Plastic wrap

1. **Cook the cream and milk.** In the medium pot, whisk together the milk, cornstarch, cream, and vanilla. Put the pot on the stove over medium-high heat. Whisking constantly, cook until the mixture heats and is thick enough to coat the back of a spoon, 5 to 10 minutes.

2. **Melt the chocolate.** Put the chocolate chips in the medium microwave-safe bowl. Microwave on high heat for 20 seconds. Take the chocolate out of the microwave, stir, and put it back in for 20 more seconds. Do this until all the chocolate is melted, 1 to 1½ minutes.

3. **Make the pudding.** Pour the cream mixture into the bowl with the melted chocolate; mix well. Cover with plastic wrap and refrigerate for 2 hours before serving.

KICK IT UP A NOTCH: Freeze the pudding in ice-pop molds; they will taste just like fudge pops.

Raspberry Frozen Yogurt

Do you fro-yo, bro? You can have ras-bo fro-yo at home, yo, whenevs. To translate: Do you enjoy the pleasure of a delicious frozen yogurt treat every now and again, friend? Well, now you can indulge whenever you'd like with this magnificent homemade raspberry frozen yogurt.

5 Ingredients, 30 Minutes, Gluten-Free, Leftover Friendly, Nut-Free, One Pot, Vegetarian

MAKES: *4 servings*

PREP TIME: *5 minutes*

1 cup frozen raspberries

1 cup plain Greek yogurt

2 tablespoons sugar

TOOLS & EQUIPMENT

Measuring spoons

Measuring cups

Food processor

1. **Puree the ingredients.** Put the raspberries, yogurt, and sugar in the food processor and puree until smooth.

2. **Serve or freeze.** Serve the frozen yogurt right away, or freeze for up to 2 months.

HELPFUL HINT: Substitute any other frozen fruit for the raspberries.

BLUEBERRY-ALMOND GALETTE

A galette is like a free-form pie. Using store-bought puff pastry makes this dish a breeze. Get creative with it and substitute apples, pears, strawberries and rhubarb, cherries, or anything else you can think of. If desired, serve this with whipped cream or ice cream.

5 Ingredients, Leftover Friendly, Vegetarian

MAKES: *6 servings*
PREP TIME: *5 minutes*
COOK TIME: *30 minutes*

4 cups frozen blueberries

2 tablespoons cornstarch

¼ cup sugar

1 sheet frozen puff pastry, defrosted

¼ cup sliced almonds

TOOLS & EQUIPMENT

Measuring spoons

Measuring cups

Knife

Wooden spoon

Medium bowl

Sheet pan

Parchment paper

1. **Preheat your oven to 400°F.** Line the sheet pan with parchment paper.

2. **Make the filling.** In the medium bowl, combine the frozen blueberries, cornstarch, and sugar.

3. **Make the galette.** Unfold and place the puff pastry on the sheet pan. Pour the blueberry mixture onto the center of the pastry, and fold the edges of the pastry up and over the fruit. Press the edges down as much as possible. Sprinkle the almonds over the blueberries.

4. **Bake the galette.** Bake the pastry for 25 to 30 minutes, until it is golden brown. Let it rest for 5 minutes before cutting into 6 pieces and serving.

Banana and Chocolate Chip Bread Pudding

Bread pudding is best when made with brioche, which is a rich egg-and-milk bread. If you can't find brioche, though, any bread will do. The key is to use stale bread. If you have to, leave the bread out, unwrapped, on your counter overnight. Fresh bread absorbs too much of the egg mixture and becomes overly saturated. Serve the pudding as is or with whipped cream or ice cream.

Leftover Friendly, Nut-Free, Vegetarian

MAKES: *6 servings*

PREP TIME: *10 minutes, plus 10 minutes to rest*

COOK TIME: *30 minutes*

1 teaspoon butter

4 large eggs

½ cup heavy cream

½ cup whole milk

¾ cup sugar

4 cups stale bread pieces

1 cup sliced banana

½ cup semisweet chocolate chips

TOOLS & EQUIPMENT

Measuring spoons

Measuring cups

Whisk

Large bowl

9-inch pie plate

Parchment paper

Aluminum foil

1. **Preheat your oven to 350°F.** Lightly butter the 9-inch pie plate.

2. **Make the custard base.** In the large bowl, whisk together the eggs, cream, milk, and sugar.

3. **Soak the bread.** Add the bread pieces to the egg mixture, making sure all the bread is moistened, and let it sit for 5 minutes.

4. **Add the remaining ingredients.** Stir in the banana and chocolate chips.

5. **Bake the bread pudding.** Pour the mixture into the prepared pie plate. Cover with parchment paper and then foil. Bake for 25 minutes. Remove the foil and parchment and bake for 5 more minutes.

6. **Rest and serve.** Let the bread pudding rest for 10 minutes, then serve.

KICK IT UP A NOTCH: For a great summer bread pudding, replace the banana with the same amount of sliced strawberries, and use white chocolate chips instead of semisweet chocolate.

MINI BERRY PAVLOVA

There's a lot of confusion about where the pavlova comes from. Australians, New Zealanders, and Russians all say they invented it. The dessert is named for the famous Russian ballerina Anna Pavlova, who traveled to all these countries to perform. Regardless of who's right, what matters is that now you get to claim this dessert as your own.

Gluten-Free, Leftover Friendly, Nut-Free, Vegetarian

MAKES: *6 servings*
PREP TIME: *35 minutes*
COOK TIME: *1 hour 25 minutes*

3 large egg whites

⅛ teaspoon kosher salt

¾ cup plus 1 tablespoon sugar

1 teaspoon cornstarch

1 cup heavy cream

1 teaspoon vanilla extract

1 cup mixed fresh berries

TOOLS & EQUIPMENT

Measuring spoons

Measuring cups

Medium bowl

Soup spoon

Spatula

Hand mixer

Sheet pan

Parchment paper

1. **Preheat your oven to 225°F.** Line the sheet pan with parchment paper.

2. **Make the meringue.** Put the egg whites in the medium bowl along with the salt. Beat with the hand mixer on medium-low speed for 2 to 3 minutes, or until the egg whites start to foam. Add ¾ cup of sugar and the cornstarch, turn the mixer up to high speed, and beat the whites for 10 minutes, until stiff.

3. **Form the pavlovas.** Use a ⅓-cup measuring cup to scoop up portions of the beaten egg whites and drop them in mounds on the lined sheet pan. Press the bowl of a soup spoon into the center of each mound to make a 2-inch depression about ½ inch deep. Wash and dry the bowl.

4. **Bake the meringues.** Put the meringues in the oven and bake for 1 hour and 25 minutes, or until they are crisp. Let the meringues cool to room temperature.

5. **Whip the cream.** In the medium bowl, combine the cream, remaining 1 tablespoon of sugar, and vanilla. Beat on high speed with the hand mixer for 3 to 4 minutes, or until the cream stands up on its own when you pull away the beaters.

6. **Fill and serve.** Spoon ¼ cup whipped cream into each pavlova. Top each with ¼ cup fresh berries and serve.

HELPFUL HINT: The bowl you beat the egg whites in must be very clean; otherwise, the whites won't whip correctly.

RICE PUDDING

You're probably thinking, "Rice pudding? What am I, a 70-year-old man?" If you are, awesome! Thanks for buying the book. If you aren't a septuagenarian, you should know that rice pudding is an underrated dessert that is a game-changer when done well. Add it to your repertoire, and you'll surprise and delight yourself and whomever you feed it to.

Gluten-Free, Leftover Friendly, Nut-Free, One Pot, Vegetarian

MAKES: *6 servings*
PREP TIME: *5 minutes*
COOK TIME: *35 minutes*

1 cup jasmine rice

1½ cups water

3 cups whole milk

½ cup sugar

½ teaspoon ground cinnamon

1 cup raisins

¼ teaspoon kosher salt

2 large egg yolks

TOOLS & EQUIPMENT

Measuring spoons

Measuring cups

Wooden spoon

Fine-mesh strainer

Medium pot with lid

1. **Make the rice.** Using the strainer, rinse the rice under cold water until the water runs clear. Put the rice in the medium pot along with the water. Bring to a boil over high heat, stirring once or twice. Turn the heat to low, stir one more time, and then put the lid on the pot and cook for 15 minutes. Remove the pot from the heat and let it sit, covered, for 5 minutes.

2. **Stir in the flavorings.** Add the milk, sugar, cinnamon, raisins, and salt to the pot with the rice. Heat over medium heat while stirring for 10 minutes until hot.

3. **Stir in the egg yolks.** Take the pot off the heat and stir in the egg yolks, one at a time. The heat from the rice will be enough to cook the yolks.

4. **Serve the rice pudding.** Serve the pudding warm, or chill it to serve later.

CRÈME CARAMEL

If you really want to charm someone, make them this. It looks and tastes like a restaurant-quality dessert, and it seems like something that should be really difficult to make. But, as you'll see, it isn't. Two things to keep in mind: You can't rush the caramel, and it's normal for some of the caramel to stick to the bottom of the ramekin.

Gluten-Free, Leftover Friendly, Nut-Free, Vegetarian

MAKES: *4 servings*

PREP TIME: *15 minutes, plus 2½ hours to set*

COOK TIME: *45 minutes*

---

1 cup sugar, divided

¼ cup water

1 large egg

1 large egg yolk

1 teaspoon vanilla extract

1 cup whole milk

1. **Preheat your oven to 350°F.**

2. **Make the caramel.** In the small pot, bring ½ cup of sugar and the water to a boil over high heat. Boil for 2 minutes, turn the heat down to medium-low, and simmer for 5 minutes, or until the sugar just starts to brown. Pour the caramel into the 4 ramekins and let cool for 10 minutes.

3. **Make the custard.** In the medium bowl, beat together the remaining ½ cup of sugar, the egg, egg yolk, and vanilla. In the medium pot, heat the milk until it is almost boiling, then whisk it into the eggs a few drops at a time. If you add the hot milk too quickly, you will scramble the eggs.

4. **Bake the custards.** Place the ramekins in a 9-by-13-inch baking dish, and carefully fill each ramekin with the egg-milk mixture. Fill the baking dish with hot water until it reaches halfway up the ramekins, then cover the entire dish with foil. Carefully put the baking dish in the oven. Bake the custards for 35 minutes, until set.

Continues ——◀

CRÈME CARAMEL Continued

TOOLS & EQUIPMENT

Measuring spoons

Measuring cups

Knife

Whisk

Small plate

Medium bowl

Small pot

Medium pot

4 (½-cup) ramekins

9-by-13-inch baking dish

Aluminum foil

Plastic wrap

5. **Chill the crème caramels.** Carefully take the ramekins out of the hot water, and let them cool at room temperature for 30 minutes. Cover with plastic wrap and chill in the fridge for 2 hours or overnight.

6. **Serve.** Dip each ramekin in a bowl of very hot water for 1 minute. Run a knife around the inside of the ramekin to release the custard from the side of the dish. Put a small plate on top of the ramekin and, holding together the plate and ramekin, flip the whole thing over. Give the ramekin a little shake, and the crème caramel should come right out onto the plate.

ESPRESSO–DARK CHOCOLATE TART

If you are serving a family-style or buffet-type meal, these little tarts are so dope. The shells come frozen as little pie plates. You just need to bake them and fill them. The chocolate-espresso filling hits that perfect balance of simplicity and awesomeness. Serve them as is, or top them with raspberries and whipped cream.

5 Ingredients, Leftover Friendly, Nut-Free, Vegetarian

MAKES: *12 mini tarts*
PREP TIME: *10 minutes, plus 30 minutes to chill*
COOK TIME: *20 minutes*

12 (3-inch) tart shells

1 cup semisweet chocolate chips

1 cup heavy cream

1 tablespoon butter

2 tablespoons brewed espresso or strong coffee

TOOLS & EQUIPMENT

Measuring spoons

Measuring cups

Whisk

Medium bowl

Medium pot

Sheet pan

1. **Prepare the tart shells.** Bake the tart shells on the sheet pan according to the package instructions. Remove the shells from the oven and let them cool.

2. **Make the filling.** Put the chocolate chips in the medium bowl. In the medium pot, combine the cream, butter, and espresso. Bring to a boil over high heat, then pour the mixture over the chocolate chips. Let the chocolate sit for 3 minutes, then whisk to blend.

3. **Make the tarts.** Pour the chocolate filling into the tart shells, then put the tarts in the fridge to chill for 30 minutes.

4. **Serve or store.** Serve chilled. Or, store the tarts in the fridge, covered, for up to 5 days.

Espresso–Dark Chocolate Tart · PAGE 163

MEASUREMENT CONVERSIONS

VOLUME EQUIVALENTS		U.S. STANDARD	U.S. STANDARD (OUNCES)	METRIC (APPROXIMATE)
LIQUID		2 tablespoons	1 fl. oz.	30 mL
		¼ cup	2 fl. oz.	60 mL
		½ cup	4 fl. oz.	120 mL
		1 cup	8 fl. oz.	240 mL
		1½ cups	12 fl. oz.	355 mL
		2 cups or 1 pint	16 fl. oz.	475 mL
		4 cups or 1 quart	32 fl. oz.	1 L
		1 gallon	128 fl. oz.	4 L
DRY		⅛ teaspoon	—	0.5 mL
		¼ teaspoon	—	1 mL
		½ teaspoon	—	2 mL
		¾ teaspoon	—	4 mL
		1 teaspoon	—	5 mL
		1 tablespoon	—	15 mL
		¼ cup	—	59 mL
		⅓ cup	—	79 mL
		½ cup	—	118 mL
		⅔ cup	—	156 mL
		¾ cup	—	177 mL
		1 cup	—	235 mL
		2 cups or 1 pint	—	475 mL
		3 cups	—	700 mL
		4 cups or 1 quart	—	1 L
		½ gallon	—	2 L
		1 gallon	—	4 L

OVEN TEMPERATURES

FAHRENHEIT	CELSIUS (APPROXIMATE)
250°F	120°C
300°F	150°C
325°F	165°C
350°F	180°C
375°F	190°C
400°F	200°C
425°F	220°C
450°F	230°C

WEIGHT EQUIVALENTS

U.S. STANDARD	METRIC (APPROXIMATE)
½ ounce	15 g
1 ounce	30 g
2 ounces	60 g
4 ounces	115 g
8 ounces	225 g
12 ounces	340 g
16 ounces or 1 pound	455 g

INDEX

ACKNOWLEDGMENTS

This book would not be possible without the love and support of my wife, Suzanne, and son, Llewyn. Thank you to my editor, Anna Pulley, for her patience and guidance. And thank you to everyone at Callisto Media, without whom this book would not exist. A special thank you to Brenda Kelly, Ian Miller, Jack and Barb Kavanaugh, and everyone else who has supported me over the years.

ABOUT THE AUTHOR

 Benjamin Kelly is a Red Seal chef and blogger from Nova Scotia, Canada. For more than 20 years he has worked in a wide variety of restaurants, from Canada's east coast to its far north.

Ben's love of food first developed when he was cooking corn chowder and shepherd's pie alongside his mother as a young child. That love grew as Ben was guided through his culinary journey by numerous chefs and teachers. Ben's passion now extends to teaching anyone who wants to learn about food and how to cook.

Today, Ben owns and operates a personal chef service and tends a successful food blog called ChefsNotes.com. You can find him on social media: @chefbenkelly.